The New York Times

FAVORITE DAY CROSSWORDS: TUESDAY

75 of Your Favorite Easy Tuesday Crosswords from *The New York Times*

Edited by Will Shortz

ST. MARTIN'S GRIFFIN ☙ NEW YORK

10 9 8 7 6 5 4

The New York Times

FAVORITE DAY CROSSWORDS: TUESDAY

Dromery

DEMAR REM

DomAzed

ARMORED

F_F

R WASTE
FR

#R+4WS FAEWTS

ACROSS

1 Solon, e.g.
5 Galvanometers measure them
9 Turkish bigwig
14 Quark's place
15 Sir's opposite
16 At full speed, as a ship
17 Burglarize
18 Forearm bone
19 Concerto movement
20 "What's more . . ."
21 Dannay-Lee sleuth
23 Knock down a notch
25 Package ___
26 Eskimos' region
29 Notice
33 Bing Crosby #1 hit
35 Officer-to-be
37 Scot's yes
38 "I've Got ___ in Kalamazoo"
39 BMW's 535i, e.g.
40 Gunslinger's command
41 Medic
42 South Pacific kingdom
43 Years and years
44 Not mono
46 Nail polish
48 A Guthrie
50 Video-store section
53 Legendary deejay
58 "Rock and Roll, Hoochie ___"
59 16th-century violin
60 Verdi villain

61 Valued fur
62 Beam fastener
63 Till bills
64 Poet Sexton
65 Gawk
66 Hatching site
67 "Omigod!"

DOWN

1 Dieter's meal
2 Do penance
3 Old Saturday Review humorist
4 Paramedic: Abbr.
5 Rabbit's foot, e.g.
6 Sears locale
7 Glass square
8 Brainy
9 Inlaid floor
10 Love affairs
11 Of sound mind
12 Trapper's ware

13 Before long
21 Emulate Dürer
22 Alpine song
24 Kind of hygiene
27 PC pic
28 Beg
30 "Nightingale" singer
31 "Sleepless in Seattle" co-star
32 Evergreens
33 Hires rival
34 "___ Plenty o' Nuttin' "
36 College V.I.P.
39 Dough
40 Have an opinion
42 Home wrecker
43 In a frenzy
45 Roof support
47 Greet brazenly
49 Bermuda, for one

51 Golfer Caponi
52 Hooked up, as oxen
53 Part of V.F.W.
54 Neglect
55 Igneous flow
56 Mrs. Jetson
57 Years and years
61 Fannie ___ (investment)

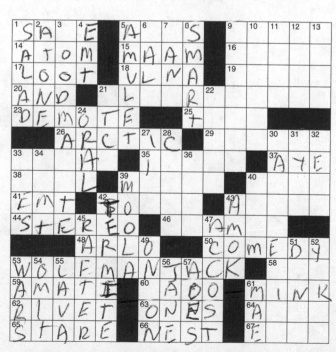

by Gregory E. Paul

2

ACROSS

1 Colorful salad ingredient
10 Plant pest
15 Throw some light on
16 El ___ (Spanish painter)
17 Acting ambassador
19 Mooring rope
20 The sky, maybe
21 Perry's creator
22 Pop's Carly or Paul
25 It's a drag
27 Country rtes.
28 It has its ups and downs
30 Turner of Hollywood
31 "Duke Bluebeard's Castle" composer
32 Super-soaked
33 Literature as art
36 Urger's words
37 Aloha State
38 Ooze
39 Bombast
40 70's sitcom "___ Sharkey"
43 Watered-down ideas
44 Subsequently
45 Teri of "Tootsie"
46 "___ Andronicus"
48 Samantha's "Bewitched" husband
50 Facetious advice in a mystery
54 Indoor design
55 Carouse
56 Birthplace of 16-Across
57 By and large

DOWN

1 ". . . for ___ for poorer"
2 Founder of est
3 Talks Dixie-style
4 Diagram a sentence
5 Competitive advantage
6 Boat's departure site
7 Rocket's departure site
8 It's after zeta
9 Foul caller
10 One more time
11 Schoolmarmish
12 Birthright
13 Bar accessory
14 ___ Passos
18 Go with the ___
22 Layup alternative
23 Quarantine
24 Be militaristic
26 Manner
28 It can sting
29 Before, in palindromes
30 Actress ___ Singer
31 Radar screen image
32 Rouse to action
33 Brief break
34 It's worth looking into
35 Clavell's "___-Pan"
36 Recipe abbr.
39 Mess-hall meal
40 Clint Eastwood's city
41 Kind of scream
42 Obstinate
44 Pelf
45 Miss Garbo
47 Jog
48 Hamlet, for one
49 Nowhere near
50 Fed. medical detectives
51 Sunny-side-up item
52 Lawyer Baird
53 Cambodia's ___ Nol

by Eric Albert

ACROSS

1 Christiania today
5 Noggin tops
10 Hind's mate
14 Hullabaloo
15 Open-eyed
16 "Damn Yankees" vamp
17 Ike was one
20 Track officials
21 Testify
22 "Rule, Britannia" composer
23 Early Briton
24 Social groups
27 Garlic relative
28 Asian holiday
31 Culture mores
32 Coxswain's crew
33 ___ Marquette
34 G.I. newspaper
37 Cures leather
38 "That's interesting"
39 Opt
40 Two-by-two vessel
41 Reared
42 Worth
43 Shed
44 Escape
45 Roman villa locale
48 Apollyon adherent
52 Biblical beacon
54 Seller's caveat
55 Backcomb hair
56 Mechanical memorization
57 Smoker's sound
58 Mead research site
59 Animal team

DOWN

1 Switch settings
2 Eye opening
3 Kind of flow
4 Bell workers
5 Thin metal disks
6 Cognizant
7 Salts
8 Dr.'s graph
9 Most rundown
10 Nodded
11 Pamplona runner
12 Hale of "Gilligan's Island"
13 10 on the Beaufort scale
18 Pressure
19 Spoon
23 Intrinsically
24 Jai alai basket
25 It makes scents
26 Part of the evening
27 Put on cargo
28 Dakota digs
29 Upright
30 Blood and acid, e.g.
32 Beginning
33 Bohemian beers
35 Berlin events of 1948
36 Recap
41 Machetelike knife
42 Wimbledon champ Gibson
43 Code name
44 1980 DeLuise flick
45 Royal Russian
46 "___ girl!"
47 Ski spot
48 Coal stratum
49 Hotcakes acronym
50 Bristle
51 Revenuers, for short
53 "___ sport"

by Joel Davajan

4

ACROSS
1 Dog star
5 Gull's cousin
9 Eyeball bender
14 Ground grain
15 Mini revelation
16 Red-eyed bird
17 Haitian despot
20 Cordwood measure
21 Jewish dance
22 Out's opposite
23 Vidal's Breckinridge
25 Actor Young of TV's 67-Across
27 Is grief-stricken
30 Book subtitled "His Songs and His Sayings"
35 Supped
36 Relative of a Bap. or Presb.
37 Balkan capital
38 Gabor sister
40 Thimbleful
42 Dryden work
43 Help get situated
45 Plugs of a sort
47 Saturn's wife
48 1956 Rosalind Russell role
50 "For ___ us a child is born"
51 Headlight?
52 Survey chart
54 Seaweed product
57 ___ fixe
59 Reached the total of
63 Popular psychologist
66 Paul Anka hit
67 See 25-Across
68 Deep blue
69 Throat malady
70 Achy
71 James Mason sci-fi role of 1954

DOWN
1 Rock band equipment
2 Usher
3 Mend, in a way
4 Alternatives to The Club
5 Round stopper
6 Delights
7 Change the décor
8 Kind of network
9 Roman breakfast?
10 Light beers
11 "Jewel Song," e.g.
12 Mariner's peril
13 Raced
18 She played Grace Van Owen on "L.A. Law"
19 Passepartout, to Phileas Fogg
24 Strongly scented plant
26 Stellar Ram
27 Fiji neighbor
28 City in northern Japan
29 Set in motion
31 Dinnerware
32 Building contractor
33 Not suitable
34 Final authority
36 Madness
39 Oust
41 Nurse, maybe
44 Directed toward a goal
46 Hair fixative
49 Office connections?
50 Donny Osmond, e.g.
53 Record-holding N.F.L. receiver ___ Monk
54 Postfixes
55 Sandpaper surface
56 Opened a crack
58 Catalonian river
60 Hawaiian hen
61 In shape
62 Kon-Tiki Museum site
64 Shrill bark
65 Lyric poem

by Janie Lyons

ACROSS

1 They're plucked
6 Busy as __
10 Lake formed by Hoover Dam
14 Bye
15 Druid, e.g.
16 Presque __, Me.
17 Close behind
20 Chair plan
21 Setter or retriever
22 "Fables in Slang" author
24 Part of a bridal bio
25 Words after "The last time I saw Paris"
34 Buck follower
35 Muddies the water
36 "The Company"
37 Bara and Negri
39 Years in Paris
40 Mole
42 Native: Suffix
43 Comedienne Fields
45 Hebrides language
46 Completely unperturbed
50 Olympian: Abbr.
51 Knock-knock joke, e.g.
52 Sounds the hour
56 1967–70 war site
61 Discourage
63 Japanese aboriginal
64 Assassinate
65 Put up
66 Cuff
67 Cod relative
68 Drinks with straws

DOWN

1 It's a laugh
2 1985 film "My Life as __"
3 __ of passage
4 Drudge
5 Dairy bar order
6 Otto's "oh!"
7 English channel, with "the"
8 Like many textbook publishers
9 Adjective for Rome
10 Cellar growth
11 Old gas brand
12 Sleep like __
13 Excellent, in slang
18 Cry of achievement
19 Ancient capital of Macedonian kings
23 Corrigenda
25 June in Hollywood
26 Sister of Thalia
27 Alfa __
28 Sock __
29 Quinine water
30 Smarten
31 Lip-puckering
32 Hair-coloring solution
33 __ et Magistra (1961 encyclical)
38 It causes sparks
41 Lapidarist's object of study
44 City on Lake Winnebago
47 Tar
48 Actor Gooding, Jr.
49 Glues
52 Earth
53 Bluefin
54 Scat cat
55 It's north of Neb.
57 Flying: Prefix
58 TV exec Friendly
59 Capa __ (westernmost point in continental Europe)
60 Colonists
61 __ de deux
62 Fork

by Ronald C. Hirschfeld

6

ACROSS

1 Rumble
6 Not fancy?
10 Difficult obligation
14 "___ of do or die"
15 Bing Crosby best seller
16 Guthrie the younger
17 Hearty entree
20 Kibbutzniks dance
21 Reverse
22 Must
23 Place to crash
25 Kipling novel
26 Tasty side dish
35 Mortgage matter
36 Words before "in the arm" or "in the dark"
37 Detective's cry
38 Them in "Them!"
39 Common key signature
40 Composer ___ Carlo Menotti
41 Cpl., for one
42 Feed a fete
43 Stood for
44 Yummy dessert
47 Cherbourg chum
48 Latin I?
49 Lamb Chop's "spokesperson"
52 Oceania republic
55 Windmill segment
59 Eventual bonus?
62 Cream-filled sandwich
63 Debouchment
64 Internet patrons
65 Blubber
66 Yeltsin veto
67 Koch's predecessor

DOWN

1 Calculator work
2 Radar blip
3 Thieves' hideout
4 They're loose
5 "Yikes!"
6 "The Afternoon of a ___"
7 In the thick of
8 First name in perfumery
9 Venture
10 Japanese mats
11 Olympic hawk
12 Bed-frame crosspiece
13 "Mikado" executioner
18 Sport whose name means "soft way"
19 Polo, e.g.
24 Circulars
25 Carpenter's woe
26 Old French bread?
27 High-priced spread?
28 ". . . and eat ___"
29 Subj. of a Clinton victory, 11/17/93
30 Key
31 Midway alternative
32 River nymph
33 The Gold Coast, today
34 "À votre ___!"
39 Java neighbor
40 Columbus, by birth
42 "Nancy" or "Cathy"
43 Puss
45 Server on skates
46 Dos + cuatro
49 Take third
50 Take on
51 "___ on Film" (1983 book set)
52 Conniving
53 Coach Nastase
54 Rock's Joan
56 Sphere
57 "Cheers" habitué
58 Alternatively
60 Lady lobster
61 Ungainly craft

by David A. Rosen

ACROSS

1 John Denver's "Christmas in ___"
6 "Tuna-Fishing" painter
10 Among
14 "___ Eyes" (1969 song)
15 Actor Richard
16 Bounty rival
17 Refinement
18 Witticisms
19 Vigor
20 1950 Sinatra hit
23 West Bank org.
24 "Just a ___"
25 Three strokes, perhaps
28 Actress Sommer
31 Shares
36 Feared test
38 Troubles
40 Weaken
41 1955 Sinatra hit
44 Improve
45 Rig
46 Shut off
47 Beachwear
49 Relax
51 Audit conductor, for short
52 Guy's date
54 Eternity
56 1961 Sinatra hit
64 "Warm"
65 Minnow eater
66 Driving hazard
68 Petruchio's mate
69 Shillelagh land
70 10th-day-of-Christmas gift
71 Swerve
72 Henna and others
73 Follow

DOWN

1 Blue-chip symbol
2 Lively dance
3 Chihuahua change
4 Bar, in law
5 Compass part
6 Half begun?
7 Excited
8 Stucco backing
9 Foot part
10 Swear
11 Ryun's run
12 Basil's successor
13 Niels Bohr, e.g.
21 The Man Without a Country
22 More aloof
25 Propels a gondola
26 Bouquet
27 Bird "perched upon a bust of Pallas"
29 Toddlers
30 Dramatist Rice
32 Goddess of discord
33 Raccoon kin
34 Lawn tool
35 Is apparent
37 Impart
39 Ditto
42 Saw
43 Elevated
48 Stood up
50 Kind of switch
53 Distrustful
55 Run site
56 Prepares the presses
57 Plumber's concern
58 Behind
59 Ale
60 Pennsylvania port
61 Roadhouses
62 They go into locks
63 Relative of Hindustani
67 Volte-face WNW

by Albert J. Klaus

8

ACROSS
1 Crocus bulb
5 "Son of the Sun"
9 Set-to
14 Pastiche
15 Score in pinochle
16 "A house is not ___"
17 Restaurant request
18 Vessel for Jill
19 "Anticipation" singer
20 Song by 11-Down
23 Vinegary
24 Scottish hillside
25 Westernmost Aleutian
27 A clef
32 Unsettle?
35 Scruff
38 "Aeneid" locale
39 Musical or song by 11-Down
42 Nobelist Wiesel
43 Rows before P
44 Gorky's "The ___ Depths"
45 Had a hunch
47 Carol
49 Daffy Duck talk
52 Bedtime annoyances
56 Song by 11-Down
61 Mercutio's friend
62 Cigar's end
63 Prefix with China
64 An acid
65 Alert
66 Ending with gang or mob
67 Guided a raft

68 Kane's Rosebud
69 Libel, e.g.

DOWN
1 Pause sign
2 Relating to $C_{18}H_{34}O_2$
3 Dyeing instruction
4 Some handlebars
5 Collision
6 Circa
7 Mountaineer
8 Psychiatrist Alfred
9 Tennessee Senator Jim
10 I.O.U.
11 Late, great composer
12 Mine: Fr.

13 "State of Grace" star
21 Thurber's Walter
22 Informal goodbye
26 Word on a coin
28 Student of animal behavior
29 Make coffee
30 Knowledge
31 Spectator
32 Farm mothers
33 Base
34 "The doctor ___"
36 Barley beard
37 Exploited worker
40 It may be golden
41 Actress Verdugo
46 Friend of Harvey the rabbit
48 Belgian port
50 Mergansers' kin

51 Perfumery bit
53 Showed allegiance, in a way
54 Downy bird
55 Stable sound
56 Envelop
57 Our genus
58 Biographer Ludwig
59 Hawaiian honker
60 To be, to Henri

by Joy L. Wouk

ACROSS

1 College digs
5 Haggadah-reading time
10 Coarse hominy
14 Piedmont city
15 Cuisine type
16 The Magi, e.g.
17 Railbird's passion
20 Certain wind
21 Check
22 Opposite of "yippee!"
23 Buyer caveat
24 Bottoms
27 Darlings
28 Railroad abbr.
31 Old toy company
32 Trim
33 It's not a dime a dozen
34 Bettor's bible
37 Grocery buy
38 Sword of sport
39 Archaic "prior"
40 Political abbr.
41 Cutting reminder?
42 Didn't quite rain
43 Broadcasts
44 Baptism, e.g.
45 Corner piece?
48 Some legal documents
52 Across-the-board bet
54 Mont. neighbor
55 Mercantilism
56 Mrs. Chaplin
57 Curaçao ingredient
58 Downy duck
59 Snoopy

DOWN

1 Desert dessert
2 Agcy. founded in 1970
3 Hwys.
4 Results of some errors
5 Summer wear
6 Some House of Lords members
7 Word before free or calls
8 Ike's command, for short
9 Double-check the seat belts
10 Muddles
11 "Judith" composer
12 Cold-war fighters
13 Starting gate
18 Like some gates
19 A Kringle
23 Penthouse home?
24 Pheasant broods
25 Words to live by
26 Stoop
27 Race-track runner
28 Snob
29 Notre planète
30 1947 Horse of the Year
32 "__ Got a Brand New Bag"
33 Track hiatus time
35 Have fun
36 Like trotters, e.g.
41 Dust collector?
42 Actor Martin
43 Dismay
44 "The Cloister and the Hearth" author
45 Switch
46 Roofing item
47 Chip in
48 Interpret
49 "Git!"
50 Geologists' times
51 Waffle
53 Dernier __

by Joel Davajan

ACROSS

1 Rig
5 Big dos
10 At a distance
14 Ur locale
15 New York's ___ Tully Hall
16 Berg opera
17 M
20 Kicker's aid
21 Names in a Saudi phone book
22 Bury
23 Cut and run
24 Yearn
26 Talk radio guest
29 Playwright O'Casey
30 Army rank, for short
33 African lily
34 Brazzaville's river
35 Through
36 H
40 Fabergé objet
41 Collection
42 Candied items
43 1969 Three Dog Night hit
44 Pup's complaints
45 Talent for cocktail talk
47 Some heirs
48 Time founder
49 "Orlando" author
52 Forum fashion
53 Quarry
56 Y
60 Organ setting
61 Type style
62 Eros
63 Ruptured
64 Tell's target
65 Currycomb target

DOWN

1 Investigate, in a way
2 Tribe whose name means "cat people"
3 Old gray animal?
4 Some ratings
5 Newgate guard
6 1966 Caine role
7 Wagons-___
8 German cry
9 Bishop's domain
10 Solo
11 Candid cameraman
12 Der ___ (Adenauer)
13 Krupp family home
18 Tall writing?
19 Tiny swimmer
23 Took off
24 Director Marshall
25 "Othello" plotter
26 Item in a locket
27 Collimate
28 Moose, e.g.
29 Divans
30 Opera prop
31 Pioneer atom splitter
32 Kingfisher's coif
34 ___ de ballet
37 Opposite of hire
38 St. Patrick's home
39 Publicity
45 Conductor Ormandy
46 Analyze verse
47 Skier's site
48 Dietary
49 ___ Point
50 "___ victory!"
51 Stink
52 Substitute
53 Cougar
54 Caddie's offering
55 Home of Jezebel
57 ___ la-la
58 School dance
59 Scottish cap

by Robert Zimmerman

ACROSS

1 Spirogyra or frog spit
5 Impression
9 Diamond protector
13 Burpee bit
14 Conclude, as negotiations
16 See 31-Across
17 Lefty celebrity relative
20 Turkish title
21 Customary practice
22 Strengthens, with "up"
23 Tugs
25 "Babes in Toyland" star, 1960
28 Head of the costume department?
30 Leonard and Charles
31 With 16-Across, former Phillies manager
34 "Queen ___ Day" (old game show)
35 Corporate abbr.
36 Have a hunch
37 Lefty artist
41 Shows one's humanity
42 Bud
43 ___ Fein
44 Voted
45 Great
46 Overwhelms with humor
48 Catch in a net
50 Pipe type
52 Highest point in Sicily
55 Course for a newcomer to the U.S.: Abbr.
57 Lament
58 Lefty actor
62 French 101 word
63 Copy of a sort
64 Noted rap artist
65 Gloomy
66 Overdecorated
67 Danson et al.

DOWN

1 Composers' org.
2 Three miles, roughly
3 Lefty President
4 Foofaraw
5 Horus's mother
6 Star in Cygnus
7 Baa maid?
8 Razor-billed bird
9 Kind of sax
10 Publican's offerings
11 Ridicule persistently
12 Is worthwhile
15 Lefty actress
18 Five-year periods
19 Refusals
24 Former Pontiac Silverdome team
26 Camden Yards team
27 Polaroid inventor
29 Lefty comedian
31 Lefty comedian
32 Continental trading group
33 Lawyer in both "Civil Wars" and "L.A. Law"
36 Student's worry
37 Roman law
38 Before, to Byron
39 Jutlander, e.g.
40 In a despicable way
45 Writer Quindlen
47 Blotto
48 $C_4H_{10}O$
49 Subs
51 Bridge seats
52 Horse that made sense?
53 One of the Jackson 5
54 Tannish color
56 Hot
59 Chaperoned girl
60 Actress Joanne
61 Paroxysm

by Peter (Lefty) Gordon

ACROSS

1 Scroogian comments
5 Grandson of Adam
9 Biblical possessive
12 Sheltered, at sea
13 Spot for Spartacus
14 Carnival ride cry
15 "Ho, ho, ho" fellow
18 Seems
19 Hockey's Bobby et al.
20 Blue Eagle initials
21 Feasted
23 "My salad days when I was ___": Shakespeare
30 Favorite dog name
31 Closes in on
32 The East
33 Word in a price
35 Volcano spew
36 Deli cry
37 Cause for liniment
38 Not-so-prized fur
40 River inlet
41 Bucky Dent slew it at Fenway Park in 1978
45 Zorba portrayer
46 Tennis call
47 Sulk angrily
48 Many Dickens stories, originally
52 Civil War currency
56 Merit
57 Nintendo hero
58 One of the Simpsons
59 Sot's problem
60 Jot
61 Prepares the dinner table

DOWN

1 Mexican peninsula
2 Crooked
3 Maids
4 Moon goddess
5 Misreckons
6 Born
7 Indivisible
8 ___ Marcos, Tex.
9 Arid region of India
10 Chick watchers
11 Thus far
13 Take with ___ of salt
14 Utility employee
16 It comes in balls
17 Bad news at a talent show
21 "Bull ___" (Costner film)
22 Psyche parts
23 Word in a monarch's name
24 Extent
25 National treasures
26 Tidy up
27 Teen heartthrob Priestley
28 Undeliverable letter, in post-office talk
29 13th-century invader
34 Monastery head
38 D.C. legislator
39 El Greco's "View of ___"
42 Nothing: Fr.
43 Pianist Peter
44 Part of rock's C.S.N. & Y.
47 Brotherhood
48 Comic bit
49 "I cannot tell ___"
50 Ultimate
51 Madrid Mmes.
52 Dropout's degree: Abbr.
53 Status letters, perhaps
54 "Say ___"
55 Dernier ___

by Jonathan Schmalzbach

ACROSS

1 "West Side Story" song
6 200 milligrams
11 Low island
14 1968 song "All __ the Watchtower"
15 River to the Missouri
16 Fuss
17 Seaver's nickname
19 Robert Morse Tony-winning role
20 House cleaner, in England
21 "Absolutely"
22 Legal profession
24 Queen Victoria's house
26 Freight charge
27 Half-wit
28 Better than a bargain
29 Polynesian carvings
33 "Hail, Caesar!"
34 Netman Nastase
37 Sheepish
38 Cup's edge
39 Battery part
40 Anti-prohibitionists
41 Disfigure
42 Get extra life from
43 Portaged
45 Patriotic uncle
47 Rocket's cargo
49 Crib-sheet contents
54 Earthy colors
55 Veneration
56 Hand-cream ingredient
57 "Harper Valley __"
58 Decorative tree
61 Sock in the jaw
62 Address grandly
63 Coeur d' __, Idaho
64 Flood relief?
65 Pave over
66 Coiffed like Leo

DOWN

1 "Concentration" objective
2 Hello or goodbye
3 Type type
4 Opening
5 Stone, for one
6 Kitchen gadgets
7 Garage-sale words
8 Spitfire fliers, for short
9 Work up
10 Electronics whiz
11 Western spoof of 1965
12 "What __" ("I'm bored")
13 "__ Sixteen" (Ringo Starr hit)
18 Package-store wares
23 Skater Zayak
25 Place for posies
26 Call back
29 Wrecker
30 "__ had it!"
31 News locale of 12/17/03
32 Shoe part
33 Auto option, informally
35 Wallet contents, for short
36 Shoebox letters
38 Alan or Cheryl
39 Kind of buildup
41 Gauge
44 Inertia
45 Finn's pal
46 Once again
47 "Where's __?" (1970 flick)
48 Part owner?
50 Half of a Western city name
51 Pulitzer-winning novelist Glasgow
52 TV exec Arledge
53 Basted
55 Cinema canine
59 __ out (missed)
60 Descartes's conclusion

by Fred Piscop

14

ACROSS
1 *Break down grammatically*
6 *Items in a still life*
11 Braincase
13 "___ Fables"
15 Considers bond values again
16 Reduce to ashes
18 Fred's sister
19 ___ Speedwagon
20 Not give ___
21 Mediocre
22 Argued
24 Loudonville, N.Y., campus
25 Classical name in medicine
27 Sprinted
28 "___ Believer" (Monkees hit)
31 Barn topper
32 Football squad
36 Court ruling
37 Hint to solving the eight italicized clues
39 ___ Jima
40 Ignite
42 Plane or dynamic preceder
43 Actress Ryan
44 Deteriorate
45 Curses
47 Sprockets linker
50 Reps.' counterparts
51 Riding whip
55 Natural gait
56 Emily, to Charlotte
57 Madrid attraction
58 Kind of lot
60 Zebralike
62 March laboriously

63 *Paired nuclides*
64 *Catch suddenly*
65 *Harvests*

DOWN
1 *Trims*
2 Kind of recording
3 Passage ceremony
4 Cash's "A Boy Named ___"
5 Printers' widths
6 Set the standard for
7 Architect Saarinen
8 Chemical suffix
9 Lettuce variety
10 *Bowling save*
11 Tomorrow: Lat.
12 Try again

14 Laurel or Musial
17 Wetlands watchdog
19 Deserters
22 Venus, for one
23 River to the Laptev Sea
24 Game fish
26 50's singer Frankie
27 Supplies with better weapons
28 Kind
29 ___ tai (cocktail)
30 Cereal bristle
33 Robust energy
34 Pronoun in a cote?
35 Norfolk ale
38 20+ quires
41 Evaporated
46 Act niggardly

47 Actor Gulager
48 Emcee
49 *Copycats*
50 More extreme
52 *Mustard plants*
53 Baltic Sea feeder
54 Pea places
56 Long account
57 Swift sailing boat
59 B-F connection
60 Salutation for Edmund Hillary
61 Half a fly

by D. J. Listort

ACROSS

1 Trounce
8 "My gal" of song
11 Castleberry of "Alice"
14 Have coming
15 Soldier's fare
17 Traveled militarily
18 Catch-22 situation
19 Black and white, e.g.
21 U.S.N. rank
22 Ireland
23 Cosmo and People, e.g.
26 I, to Claudius
27 "___ Lisa"
31 Shower mo.
32 Scruggs of bluegrass
34 Epithet for a tyrant
36 Not a warm welcome
39 Flower child
40 A big blow
41 Maupassant's "___ Vie"
42 Some of Wordsworth's words
43 Legendary Hollywood monogram
44 Ed of "Daniel Boone"
45 Roller coaster cry
47 "Society's Child" singer Janis ___
49 Sang-froid
56 In progress
57 Vegetarian's no-no
59 Alley of "Look Who's Talking"
60 Rodeo ropes
61 Ship's heading
62 Always, poetically
63 Majority's choice

DOWN

1 S. & L. offerings
2 Lover's
3 Christiania, today
4 Scarlett and others
5 Bear Piccolo
6 Civil rights leader Medgar
7 Change the décor
8 Punic War general
9 Knight's attire
10 Slip-up
11 Fight sight
12 Mislay
13 Washington bills
16 Mai ___
20 Like Captain Ahab
23 Like a he-man
24 Sap sucker
25 Bellyache
26 Be off the mark
27 Denver summer time: Abbr.
28 Disgrace
29 Nary a person
30 Saint whose feast day is January 21
32 Biblical judge
33 Word of support
34 Bugs's voice
35 Hairy ancestor
37 Obsolescent disks
38 Engine part
43 Like slim pickings
44 Lacking iron, maybe
45 Essayist E. B.
46 Three-time skating gold medalist
47 Model
48 Novelist Malraux
49 Furnace fuel
50 Getting ___ years
51 Bogeyman
52 Pop music's ___ Lobos
53 Gardner of mysteries
54 Backside
55 Overindulge
58 Chairman's heart?

by Harvey Estes

16

ACROSS
1 Colo. acad.
5 Start fishing
9 "Dancing Queen" pop group
13 Mata __
14 Tear to shreds
16 Tactic
17 Singer Antoine from New Orleans
19 Intense anger
20 Carty of baseball
21 __ and kin
23 "The Company"
24 Mister twister
28 San Francisco area
29 Antitoxins
30 Laughed, in a way
32 Transfer, as a legal proceeding
36 "Tie a Yellow Ribbon" tree
37 Native land
39 Inform (on)
40 Fantasized
44 Durante's "Mrs."
48 Cosmonaut Gagarin
50 1956 Oscar-winning actress
51 Birthday-suit activity
55 One of L.B.J.'s dogs
56 Munich's river
57 Max or Buddy
59 Till compartment
61 Film hit of 1934
65 Dermatologist's diagnosis
66 Underwater acronym
67 Tevye portrayer on stage
68 Feminist Millett
69 Mikulski and Murkowski: Abbr.
70 Once more

DOWN
1 TV initials
2 Region of heavy W.W. II fighting
3 Heart of the grocery?
4 Champion named 9/1/72
5 __-Magnon
6 Goal
7 Acerbic
8 Acropolis attire
9 Bank loan abbr.
10 Longtime Supreme Court name
11 Humphrey, to Bacall
12 TV's "__ in the Life"
15 Commotion
18 Act like the Apostle Thomas
22 "__ goes!"
25 __ Harbour, Fla.
26 Playoff breathers
27 Machine part
28 "__ she blows!"
30 Food fish
31 A dwarf
33 Syracuse players
34 Floral container
35 Biblical suffix
38 Moist
41 Novelist Rand
42 City bond, for short
43 Secret lovefests
45 Appearance at a sit-down?
46 Suspect's "out"
47 Top-rated TV show of the 60's
49 Baking potatoes
51 Kind of therapy
52 Mol's country
53 "__ my case"
54 "Goodnight __"
58 Steak order
60 Marie, e.g.: Abbr.
62 Aruba product
63 Nolte's "48 __"
64 Right away

by David J. Kahn

ACROSS

1 Caspar or Balthazar, e.g.
6 Rope material
10 Chorale part
14 Florida city
15 Jai ___
16 La Scala presentation
17 NO UNTIDY CLOTHES
20 Walking on air
21 Macadam ingredient
22 ___ Cruces, N.M.
23 Prepared
24 Harem
26 Claus Subordinate
29 Apocalypse
31 Gene material
32 Seldom seen
34 "QB VII" author
36 Lump of jelly, e.g.
39 GOVERN, CLEVER LAD
43 "You said it!"
44 Writer Shere
45 Approve
46 W.W. II grp.
48 Agrippina's son
50 German pronoun
51 Answer to "What's keeping you?"
55 Mount near ancient Troy
57 Item in a lock
58 "I" affliction
59 1990 Bette Midler film
62 BLATHER SENT ON YE
66 Neighborhood
67 Le Mans, e.g.
68 Conductor Georg
69 Back-to-school time: Abbr.
70 Bouquet
71 Friend of Henry and June

DOWN

1 Word on the Oise
2 Long (for)
3 Food critic Greene
4 Arm bones
5 Fried lightly
6 Actor Charles of "Hill Street Blues"
7 Overhead trains
8 Not shiny
9 A captain of the Enterprise
10 Dance, in France
11 On ___ (doing well)
12 1979 treaty peninsula
13 Authority
18 Alternate road
19 Los Angeles suburb
24 Obviously pleased
25 Big name in viniculture
26 Physics unit
27 Zhivago's love
28 "It Came ___ Outer Space"
30 Mezz. alternative
33 "It's true," in Torino
35 French resort town
37 Forest florae
38 ___ B'rith
40 Fingernail polish
41 Realism
42 Salon selection
47 Rossini character
49 Potemkin mutiny site
51 Jots
52 Skiing's Phil or Steve
53 Tiptoe
54 Air Force arm: Abbr.
56 Illinois city
59 Cassandra
60 Falana or Montez
61 Opposing
63 Dracula, sometimes
64 Sgt., e.g.
65 Frozen Wasser

by Stephanie Spadaccini

18

ACROSS

1 Actress Winger
6 Park, in Monopoly
11 "Honest" fellow
14 Where Gauguin visited van Gogh
15 Funnyman O'Brien
16 Bloodshot
17 "Cheers!" in Cherbourg?
19 Chang's Siamese twin
20 Brand of lemon-flavored drink
21 Daydream
23 Koch and Wynn
24 Pampering, for short
26 It's heard in a herd
27 Garibaldi in Genoa?
33 Pickle
36 Subject for a supermarket tab
37 Avaricious one
38 October gem
40 Beam fastener
42 1963 Oscar winner
43 Arose
45 Danger
47 Hang in the breeze
48 Madrid's equivalent of a Texas university?
50 Performance
51 Had lunch
52 Montana and Moon, in brief
55 Gladstone rival
60 Real
62 "Poppycock!"
63 Pre-photo pronouncement in Geneva?
65 Some
66 Skirmish
67 "Dallas" Miss
68 Simonize
69 Classic theater name
70 4-Down again

DOWN

1 Peri opera
2 Made a boner
3 Post-sneeze word
4 Take money for a spare room
5 Loner
6 Agt.'s share
7 Creator of Lorelei Lee
8 Med. subj.
9 Winter melon
10 Competitor
11 Vicinity
12 Early German carmaker
13 Barely beat, with "out"
18 Woman's top
22 Cartoonist Wilson
25 Islamic leader
28 Crowbar
29 Portugal and its neighbor
30 Barely managed, with "out"
31 Raise
32 Alternative to Charles de Gaulle
33 Clinton's runs
34 Each
35 First name in spying
39 Moon-based
41 Alternative to Certs
44 "Desmoiselles d'Avignon" artist
46 Bloodletting practitioner
49 Potted
52 Put down
53 Count in music
54 Winter weather
55 Extract
56 New Rochelle college
57 Charon's domain
58 Kind of beer
59 Relationship words
61 Prefix with play or scope
64 Favorite relative in politics?

by Mark Danna

ACROSS
1 Zubin with a baton
6 Old streetlight
13 Daley and others
14 Gravel-voiced actress
15 Iron shortage
16 Commit
17 Just the highlights
18 Slammin' Sam
19 Trendy
20 Getting better, as wine: Var.
22 Up to now
24 Size up
26 Paints amateurishly
28 Almost shut
32 Kind of symbol
33 One whom Jesus healed
34 Rodeo rope
35 Dashboard reading, for short
36 Leave the pier
38 Acquire
39 Ask on one's knees
41 Had
42 Lunch order
43 Belgrade dweller
44 In abeyance
45 Sciences' partner
46 Tooth
48 Comfort
50 Probe
53 Some pads
55 Accident mementos
58 Serves a sentence
60 Byrnes, on "77 Sunset Strip"
61 Brown paint, e.g.
62 Six-footer?
63 Resort locale
64 Newspaper section

DOWN
1 Lion's pride?
2 It's hard to miss
3 Respect
4 Nonsense
5 Simile center
6 Comic Kaplan
7 Assuages
8 Picture with its own frame
9 Wheel bolt holder
10 King of comedy
11 Part of a pair
12 Sound of relief
13 Scuff up
14 It's hard to say
18 Fastens with a pop
21 "I have no ___!"
23 ___ chi ch'uan
24 Tail ends
25 Temptation for Atalanta
27 1991 American Conference champs
29 It's hard
30 Listing
31 Sounds off
33 Digital-watch readout: Abbr.
34 Postal letters
37 Have a hunch
40 1970 Jackson 5 hit
44 Looking while lusting
45 Waylay
47 Time and again
49 In unison
50 Tots up
51 Afternoon TV fare
52 Lifetime Achievement Oscar winner Deborah
54 Mingo portrayer
56 Puerto ___
57 Play place
59 Take part in a biathlon
60 Kipling novel

by Harvey Estes

ACROSS

1 Swiss city on the Rhine
6 "Jake's Thing" author
10 Nice shindigs
14 Allan-___ (Robin Hood cohort)
15 Carry on
16 "___ Fire" (Springsteen hit)
17 *Paris site*
18 "___ partridge in a . . ."
19 Kind of fountain
20 Runaway, of a sort
22 Runaway, of a sort
24 Book-lined rooms
25 *London site*
27 Cartoonist Bushmiller
29 Twofold
32 Game award, for short
35 Make a pot
36 Skin layer
38 *Rome site*
40 *Amsterdam site*
41 Drop out
42 Seat for two or more
43 "You don't ___!"
44 ___-tiller
45 They beat deuces
47 *Florence site*
50 Not on land
54 Upset-minded teams
57 Positions
59 Big 10's ___ State
60 Letter encl.
62 *Moscow site*
63 Derby

64 Ended
65 Off
66 River to the North Sea
67 Corn bread
68 Having an irregular edge

DOWN

1 With ___ breath
2 One of the Astaires
3 Dresden dweller
4 Slip by
5 ___ majesty
6 Mr. Parseghian
7 Sea cow
8 Kipling story locale
9 Legendary Packers QB
10 Surgical knife
11 Love, Spanish-style
12 Italian town, site of a 1796 Napoleon victory
13 Fastener
21 N.F.L. standout Lott
23 Not a main route
26 Naldi of silents
28 1964 Four Seasons hit
30 "___ 'n' Andy"
31 Trevi Fountain coin
32 Classic sports cars
33 Turn sharply
34 Somewhat, in music
36 Loss
37 High overhead?
39 Money for Mason

40 "Cheers" role
42 Harold of politics
46 Pianist Gyorgy
48 Noted children's writer
49 An encouraging word
51 Defunct treaty org.
52 Group character
53 Unanimously
54 Nimble
55 Birds Eye product
56 ___-over
58 "___ kleine Nachtmusik"
61 Afore

by Ernie Furtado

ACROSS

1 Clicker that might be used on a trawler?
9 London elevator
13 Tibetan V.I.P.
14 Plume source
16 Starter at an Italian restaurant
17 Quick on one's toes
18 Shoshonean
19 Health resort
20 Department store employee
21 Behan's "___ Boy"
23 George Sand, e.g.
24 Gene Kelly's "___ Girls"
25 Loving touches
26 German coal region
28 Propelled a punt
29 Amtrak listing: Abbr.
30 One of the Astors
31 Is interested
32 Caddies carry them
33 Bank account amt.
34 Vatican City dwellers
35 Jetty
36 It causes a reaction
38 Great noise
39 Sparta was its capital
40 Have the chair
44 Resounding, as a canyon
45 TV knob abbr.
46 Statehouse V.I.P.
47 Left the chair
48 Cheese at an Italian restaurant
51 "Put up your ___!"
52 Relinquishes
53 Élan
54 Solemn hymn

DOWN

1 Piece of a poem
2 Change, as hems
3 Capuchin monkey
4 Racetrack informant
5 Confirmation slaps
6 Twangy
7 Ambulance attendant: Abbr.
8 Philosopher's universal
9 Scholarly
10 Eliza's 'enry
11 Chicken dish
12 Distance gauge
13 Paint unskillfully
15 Brewer and Wright
20 Parisian papas
22 Kill, as a dragon
23 Turns white
25 Meltdown areas
26 City south of Palo Alto
27 Salad ingredient
28 ___ New Guinea
30 Throw off the scent
31 Some lose sleep over it
32 Baking pans
34 Most runtlike
35 Polish dumpling
37 Yankee great Skowron et al.
38 Herds
40 Call up
41 Jim Croce's "___ Name"
42 Gift getter
43 Holiday nights
48 Cushion
49 Baseball hitter's stat
50 Household god in Roman myth

by Bob Sefick

22

ACROSS

1 Kindergarten instruction
5 Onetime La Scala tenor
11 Shake up
14 Brook
15 Unlocked
16 Hollywood's Thurman
17 Star of "The Invisible Man"
19 Hoover, for one
20 Zeus or Jupiter, e.g.
21 School grp.
22 Wood-shaping tool
23 Fleur-de-___
25 Mr. Sondheim
27 Not left in the lurch
32 "The Time Machine" people
33 Speckled horse
34 Poet Wilfred
36 Meanies
39 Religious offshoot
40 Pay by mail
42 Onetime Texaco rival
43 Not on the level
45 Talkative Barrett
46 Prefix with -plasm
47 Not cleric
49 Two-pointer, the hard way
51 Comes out
54 Kin of calypso music
55 Beats it
56 Piggie
58 Orientals, e.g.
63 Belief
64 Star of "The Vanishing" (1993 version)

66 Bedlam site
67 Spoke from the soapbox
68 Pull off a coup
69 Author Beattie
70 Choir voices
71 Minus

DOWN

1 Electrical paths
2 Gyp
3 Ali, once
4 Coin that's not a coin
5 One who shares a masthead billing
6 ___ financing (car ad phrase)
7 Sow's opposite
8 Rightmost column

9 A century in Washington
10 ___ bodkins
11 Star of "Without a Trace"
12 Flabbergast
13 Japanese noodle soup
18 Kewpie
22 Orbiting points
24 Betsy Ross, e.g.
26 "Don't Bring Me Down" rock band
27 Nocturnal bear?
28 They might be heard a thousand times
29 Star of "Missing"
30 All broken up
31 Disband, postwar
35 Hirschfeld hides them

37 This, in Madrid
38 Chimney grit
41 Ale mugs
44 Barrister's headgear
48 The "c" in etc.
50 Actress Lemmons
51 "My Fair Lady" lady
52 Stoneworker
53 Divans
57 Newts
59 False god
60 Dickensian chill
61 Eerie loch
62 Concorde et al.
64 Book after Esther
65 A stingy fellow?

by David Ellis Dickerson

ACROSS

1 Whip end
5 Mystery writer's award
10 Sassy young 'un
14 "___ silly question . . ."
15 Painter Andrea del ___
16 Portnoy's creator
17 Hmm?
20 ___ Dame
21 Packwood, for one
22 Curse
25 Purse fastener
26 Jeweler's weight
28 Some of the Brady bunch
31 Eat like a chicken
34 Blend
36 Utah's Hatch
37 D.D.E.'s command
38 Hmm . . .
40 Volga tributary
41 Writer Terkel
43 Requisite
44 Porch adjunct
45 Arab capital
46 Ignoramus
48 South African statesman Jan
51 Gospel singer Jackson
55 Many TV shows
57 Cathedral displays
58 Hmm!
61 Mitch Miller's instrument
62 Mountain nymph
63 Electricity carrier
64 District

65 Don Knotts won five
66 Actress Young

DOWN

1 Suburban greenery
2 Seeing ___ (since)
3 Do figure eights
4 Where to hang your chapeau
5 Biblical verb ending
6 "Zip-a-Dee-Doo-___"
7 Alum
8 Relics collect here
9 The "R" in H.R.H.
10 Pugilistic muscleman
11 Famous debater

12 Rat chaser?
13 Talese's "Honor ___ Father"
18 Word repeated after "Que"
19 Speaker
23 In a line
24 Eagle's nail
27 Like Neptune's trident
29 Adidas rival
30 Break sharply
31 Annoyance
32 Famous last words
33 Camp V.I.P.
35 Concert hall
38 Debate subjects
39 Irish novelist O'Brien
42 Like a golf ball
44 Manatees

47 Word sung twice before "cheree"
49 Lake near Carson City
50 Drang's partner
52 DeVito's "Taxi" role
53 Venous opening
54 Gray
55 Ms. McEntire
56 Cherry leftover
58 "Far out!"
59 Spring time
60 Gains for O. J.

by Lois Sidway

ACROSS

1 Masquerades
6 "Fe, fi, fo, ___!"
9 Batman foe, with "The"
14 Native Alaskan
15 Prince Hirobumi
16 Sheeplike
17 Irving's "A Prayer for Owen ___"
18 The lambada, once
19 Grand mountain
20 Dr. Seuss title
23 Actress Skye
24 Ho Chi ___
25 Car job
28 ___ Bingle (Crosby)
30 God Almighty
34 A year in Mexico
35 Put to the grindstone
37 Studio prop
38 Dr. Seuss title
41 Plant seeds again
42 ___-scarum
43 Coach Parseghian
44 Shakespearean oath
46 Smidgen
47 Love of Greece?
48 Dance or hairstyle
50 Calf's meat
52 Dr. Seuss title
59 One-___ (short play)
60 Crystal ball, e.g.
61 Keep busy
62 Violinist Isaac
63 Part of R.S.V.P.
64 Wrestling's ___ the Giant
65 Western film title of '75 and '93
66 Golf peg
67 Relaxes

DOWN

1 Like venison
2 Out of the wind
3 Carroll contemporary
4 Em, e.g.
5 Pen, for Pierre
6 About mid-month, with "the"
7 Brigham Young's home
8 Computer-phone link
9 Norse land of giants
10 Make out at a party?
11 Songstress Eartha
12 Organic compound
13 Philosopher Descartes
21 Conclude with
22 Small bird
25 Dens
26 Hungry
27 Idaho city
29 Betty Ford program
31 1991 Stallone comedy
32 Brain surgeon's prefix
33 Columnist Maxwell et al.
35 Author from Salem, Mass.
36 Inferable
39 Dinner chickens
40 More like Shirley Temple
45 ___ Solo of "Star Wars"
47 Sir Galahad's mother
49 Popular word game
51 "___ is Born"
52 Fastener
53 VIII, to Virgil
54 Blvds. and rds.
55 Toledo's vista
56 Hitches
57 William of "The Doctor"
58 Unlocks, in a sonnet

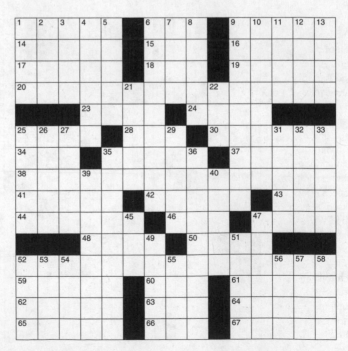

by David Ellis Dickerson

ACROSS

1 On the ___ (very angry)
8 For the well-to-do
15 November winner
16 Savannah's place
17 "Evil Ways" band
18 Bar members
19 Dynamite's kin
20 Christian Science founder
22 Pope's "An ___ on Man"
23 ___ way (incidentally)
25 Murals and the like
26 Free-for-all
29 Play callers
31 Ill-fated sibling rival
35 Put on a pedestal
36 Ark builder
37 Singer Falana
38 String player
40 "Hop to it!"
42 Cancer's symbol
43 Reds' Rose
45 2:1, e.g.
46 "A-one and ___"
47 "I smell ___"
48 TV pitchman Merlin
49 "A Christmas Carol" boy
51 Student of optometry?
53 Edinburgh dwellers
56 Aloe ___ (lotion ingredient)
57 Retirement kitty, for short
60 Evangeline, e.g.

62 Last-place finisher, so it's said
65 Unyielding
66 Fence in
67 Reneges
68 Quotes poetry

DOWN

1 Frontierward
2 Chester Arthur's middle name
3 Monthly due
4 %: Abbr.
5 ___ loss for words
6 Belief
† 7 Edith + Holly
8 Hideous
9 Black-eyed one, perhaps
10 Farmer, in the spring
† 11 Billy + Lucille
12 "Rock of ___"
13 Italian bread
14 Word before come and go
21 Car for test-driving
† 23 Alexander + Timothy
24 Abominable Snowman
25 Tennis's Arthur
26 Islamic center
27 Bring to bear
28 Steven Bochco TV drama
30 Patti + Lana
32 Boxing matches
33 Borden bovine
34 Instructions to Macduff
39 Lunch meat

41 "Star Trek" counselor
44 Record
50 Basketball's Thomas
52 "Common Sense" author
53 "Saint Joan" playwright
54 Sign over
55 Reverend Roberts
56 Animal docs
57 "___ You Babe"
58 Misleading move
59 Senate votes
61 SSW's reverse
63 New Deal grp.
64 Yale player

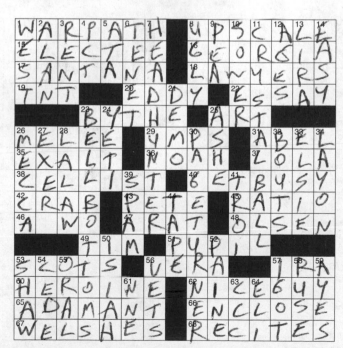

by Harvey Estes

ACROSS

1 Razor sharpener
6 Health resort
9 More than a mere success
14 Mussolini's notorious son-in-law
15 Assist
16 With uneven gait
17 Mink's poor cousin
18 Ushered
19 Truism
20 Item to cut for dessert
23 Late-night star
24 President Manuel, ousted by Franco
25 TV rooms
26 New Rochelle institution
28 Game show sound
30 Princess Diana's family name
33 Bedecked
37 Mea ___
38 Get repeated value from
39 Replaceable shoe parts
42 Agrees
44 Carry-on
45 30's and 40's actress Anna
46 Porcine cry
49 Kind of system
51 Weakens
55 Popular poultry entree
58 ___ hilt (fully)
59 "Le veau ___" ("Faust" aria)
60 Roomy dress cut
61 Chef's attire

62 Consume
63 Noted name in Bosnian talks
64 Oceans, to Longfellow
65 Season on the Riviera
66 Lawn tool

DOWN

1 "Bad mood" look
2 Small obligation
3 Snitch about
4 Entree for a solitary diner
5 Scrutinize, with "over"
6 Marathoner Alberto
7 Michelangelo work
8 Afterthoughts

9 Bridge desideratum
10 Dieter's dish
11 A miss's equivalent
12 Dish's companion in flight
13 Songs of glory
21 Diminish
22 Foray
27 Florida city
29 Like Eric the Red
30 H.S. subject
31 So-called "lowest form of wit"
32 Bygone trains
34 Sally Field TV role
35 Erhard's training
36 ___ Plaines, Ill.
40 Prefer follower
41 Latecomer to a theater, maybe

42 Ancient fertility goddess
43 Suffix with young or old
46 Santa's reindeer, e.g.
47 "___ you're happy!"
48 Potassium salt
50 Summer ermine
52 Geriatric process
53 ___ de León
54 Lip curl
56 Understands
57 Pan's opposite

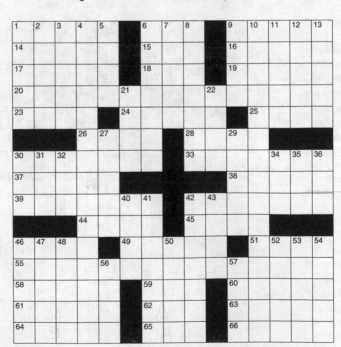

by Arthur S. Ash

ACROSS

1 Cremona violinmaker
6 Henri's squeeze
10 Tennis units
14 Quarrel
15 Stadium protests
16 Wynken, Blynken and Nod, e.g.
17 Criticize a prizefight?
19 Small brook
20 Transgression
21 Blackmailed
22 Cold stick
24 Le Sage's "Gil ___"
25 One way to run
26 Instruments for Rostropovich
29 Economic hostility
33 Poet T. S.
34 Trumpeter Al
35 ___ morgana (mirage)
36 Highway caution
37 Skater Sonja
38 Late king of Norway
39 "I ___ Got Nobody" (20's hit)
40 Mare's feed
41 Jacques, in song
42 Rings loudly
44 Bell's signal
45 Itineraries: Abbr.
46 Handed-down stories
47 Expensive
50 Bit
51 Word with date or process
54 Imitator Little
55 Boxing commission?
58 Medicinal plant
59 Killer whale
60 "Happy Birthday" medium
61 Cravings
62 Shade of blue
63 Cup of thé

DOWN

1 Clumsy boats
2 Actor Paul
3 Ever and ___
4 Idiosyncrasy
5 Imagination tester
6 French clergymen
7 "___ Indigo"
8 Chit
9 Guesswork
10 How hard Riddick Bowe can hit?
11 Rock star Clapton
12 Cash drawer
13 Fileted fish
18 "What a pity!"
23 Delivery letters
24 Items used in "light" boxing?
25 "Mrs. ___ Goes to Paris"
26 Actor Romero
27 "Dallas" matriarch Miss ___
28 Detroit footballers
29 Hues
30 Charles's princedom
31 Old name in game arcades
32 "Nevermore" quoter
34 Call at a coin flip
37 Winnie-the-pooh receptacle
41 Awhile
43 Shoshonean
44 Humorist Lazlo
46 Not an express
47 Devoutly wish
48 Annoy
49 Religious image
50 Peruvian Indian
51 Speaker's spot
52 Coffee dispensers
53 Fisher's "Postcards From the ___"
56 Suffix with fail
57 Wood sorrel

by Roger H. Courtney

ACROSS

1 Dogpatch's creator
5 Palindromic term of address
9 Talked, old-style
14 Nose tweaker
15 Willa Cather's "One of ___"
16 With sickly pallor
17 Dream
18 Till's bills
19 Rags-to-riches writer
20 Start of an old motto
22 List ender
23 Shooter ammo
24 Part 2 of motto
26 Take-___ (accompaniers)
29 ___ of one's own medicine
30 Part 3 of motto
31 Bulldog
32 Twosome
36 Martinique, e.g.
37 Environmentally minded, for short
39 Hook shape
41 "Don't Bring Me Down" rock group
42 Miami's county
44 Blanche in "The Golden Girls"
46 Part 4 of motto
48 Particle
50 Conquering hero
51 Part 5 of motto
54 Aerialist's safeguard
55 Theater people
56 End of motto
61 Sightseeing sight
62 Golfer Isao ___
63 Singleton
64 Ball
65 A night in Paris
66 Exterior: Prefix
67 Blackthorn shrubs
68 1949 erupter
69 Creep through the cracks

DOWN

1 Search thoroughly
2 Together, musically
3 On hold
4 Make believe
5 Health
6 Godmother, often
7 Rings of color
8 Orig. texts
9 Mower's trails
10 Mouth parts
11 White, informally
12 Last name in fashion
13 Nest for 21-Down: Var.
21 See 13-Down
22 "Me" types
25 Thumb-twiddling
26 Fatty ___
27 Refrain part
28 1985 Danielle Steel best seller
33 Regretfulness
34 Choir voice
35 Koh-i-___ (famed diamond)
38 Pinch reaction
40 Cut of meat
43 Nitty-gritty
45 Just managed
47 Streets
49 Medea's ill-fated uncle
51 Miss Muffet edible
52 Business as ___
53 Zoo heavyweight
57 Related
58 Comic Rudner
59 Spot
60 "Avast!"
62 Actress Sue ___ Langdon

by Ernie Furtado

ACROSS

1 Mercury or Mars
4 Good old boy
9 Double-crosser
14 1979 film "Norma ___"
15 W.W. I battle site
16 Pomme de ___ (French potato)
17 Modern bank "employee": Abbr.
18 "___ in Venice"
19 Feeling regret
20 Night photographer's work, with "a"?
23 Common connectors
24 Bother
25 Wears well
27 Kind of budget
32 Dustin, in "Midnight Cowboy"
33 Actress Ward of "Sisters"
34 Exist
35 Like an inept photographer's subject?
39 Christina's dad
40 Snoop Doggy Dogg songs
41 Ploys
42 Indy and Daytona
45 Classified
46 Sleep stage: Abbr.
47 Family member
48 Photojournalists' choices?
54 "___ Paradiso" (1966 film)
56 Catalyst
57 Mining area
58 "___ of robins in her hair"
59 San ___, Calif.
60 Chemical suffix
61 Mill, to a cent
62 Embellish
63 ___ Guinea

DOWN

1 Fat, in France
2 Vow
3 Floor model
4 Owing to
5 Defeats
6 Imps
7 One of the March sisters
8 Netman Arthur
9 Road, in Roma
10 Reflex messenger
11 Composer Satie
12 Prince Valiant's son
13 Fraternity party staple
21 "Jerusalem Delivered" poet
22 ___ Lama
25 Author Esquivel
26 Greek
27 Computer sounds
28 Swiss range
29 Trigger
30 Fumbled
31 Grades below the curve
32 Surf sound
33 Open carriage
36 Chaplin persona
37 Shadow-y surname?
38 ___-frutti
43 One of the Gallos
44 Affluence
45 Spoiler
47 Vinegar: Prefix
48 British gun
49 Lady of Spain
50 "Holy moly!"
51 Unrestricted
52 Supreme Court complement
53 Brood
54 Topper
55 Single

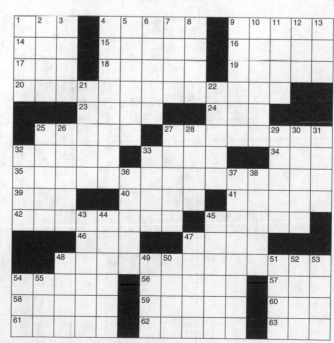

by Jonathan Schmalzbach

ACROSS

1 Incarcerate
5 Wife, in Madrid
11 U.S./U.K. divider
14 Wearer of an aiguillette
15 Warehouse charge
17 Start of a quip
19 Slippery swimmer
20 Axis end
21 Lift, as ice or oysters
22 Ilk
23 Enormous
26 Stress
29 "McSorley's Bar" painter John
30 Good earth
31 New Zealand native
32 Family V.I.P.'s
35 Middle of the quip
39 Pigpen
40 Brainy group
41 Something to cop
42 Mork's gal
43 Like schlock
45 Extra leaves
48 Ireland's ___ Islands
49 Spread for a spread
50 Manchurian border river
51 Sunny day production
54 End of the quip
59 Starlet's hope
60 Lackawanna's partner in railroads
61 Draft agcy.

62 Dallas's ___ Plaza
63 Become tiresome

DOWN

1 Rib
2 Yorkshire river
3 Worshiped one
4 Rock's ___ Zeppelin
5 Police accompaniment
6 Clown's prop
7 Corn bread
8 Assn.
9 Writer Rohmer
10 Farming: Abbr.
11 "Flow gently, sweet ___": Burns
12 Coming-of-age period

13 Shelf
16 Consumed
18 "___ the Roof" (1963 hit)
22 It's good for the long haul
23 Actress Massey
24 Filipino
25 Hotel housekeeper
26 Pauper's cry
27 Old feller
28 Guinea pig
29 Impertinent
31 Obeys
32 House slipper
33 Lincoln and Vigoda
34 Dog command
36 Head of Abu Dhabi
37 Shipped

38 Unguarded, as a receiver
42 Reagan Attorney General
43 Like a curmudgeon
44 Mata ___
45 Bridge declaration
46 D.E.A. workers
47 Swizzles
48 Provide divertissement
50 Soviet spy Rudolf
51 Now's partner
52 Siberia's site
53 River of Flanders
55 Proof's ending
56 Half of deux
57 Seventh Greek letter
58 Like a crescent moon

by Betty Jorgensen

31

ACROSS

1 Send a Dear John letter
5 Antarctica's ___ Coast
10 Stain on Santa
14 Medicinal herb
15 "Golden" song
16 Transportation Secretary Federico
17 Prefix with bucks or bytes
18 Ad: Part 1
20 Ad: Part 2
22 And others
23 Lennon's lady
24 Clinches
25 Ad: Part 3
28 Ad: Part 4
33 Beats
34 Judge
35 Dogpatch diminutive
36 Cabbies' credentials: Abbr.
37 Jabbed
38 Radio knob
39 And so forth, for short
40 Singular person
41 Gladiator's place
42 Medium in which this puzzle's ad appeared
45 Furnishes for a time
46 Twilights, poetically
47 Richmond was its cap.
48 Queen Victoria's husband
51 Ad: Part 5
55 Sponsor of the ad
57 Snead and Spade
59 15 miles of song
60 Floor pieces
61 Wasatch Range state
62 Prepared to drive
63 Unclogs
64 Glazier's section

DOWN

1 Predicament
2 "___ a song go. . . ."
3 CBS's eye, e.g.
4 Genteel snack spots
5 Topper's first name
6 Wings
7 Peculiar: Prefix
8 Clear
9 Downcast
10 Quite an impression
11 Trompe l'-___
12 "Dedicated to the ___ Love"
13 Noted Chaplin follower
19 Shoshoneans
21 Responsibility
24 Buries
25 Shiftless one
26 ___ Bandito of commercials
27 New Mexico's state flower
28 Offenses
29 "The Old ___ Bucket"
30 Martian or Venusian
31 Article of food
32 Actress Raines and others
37 Indicates
38 Concocts
41 In addition
43 Adjudged
44 "Buona ___" (Italian greeting)
47 Judit Polgar's game
48 Help a crook
49 Bait
50 Spreadable cheese
51 Tempest
52 Browning locale
53 "Do I dare to ___ peach?": Eliot
54 Muscat's land
56 Fashionable
58 That girl

by Jonathan Schmalzbach

32

ACROSS

1 "St. John Passion" composer
5 In vogue
9 Carpet variety
13 Nepal's location
14 Leftovers dish
15 Prowess
16 "Lost Horizon" paradise
18 Public sentiment
19 "Message received"
20 Songwriter John
21 Long, deep bow
25 More than a snack
27 First look
30 1901 Churchill novel, with "The"
34 With masts fully extended
35 Imprint on glass
37 Posted
38 Puny pup
39 Dweller in Gulliver's Houyhnhnmland
40 Wash
41 Deuce topper
42 Skater Heiden
43 Idolater
44 Snow remover?
46 Seven Cities of Cibola seeker
48 George Takei TV/movie role
50 Confuses
51 Shore bird
54 Soprano Nixon
57 Dik Browne Viking
58 Town visited by Tommy Albright
63 Subtle twist
64 Like elbowing, e.g.
65 Paris landing site
66 Aromatic herb
67 Prepared brandy
68 Start for "of honor" or "of silence"

DOWN

1 ___ relief
2 Ski wood
3 "The Company"
4 Solo of "Star Wars"
5 Plating material
6 Nixon chief of staff
7 Sunny vacation spot
8 Mojo
9 King Kong's home
10 Saber handle
11 To boot
12 ___ Burnie, Md.
15 Aborigine's weapon
17 Woodworker's concern
21 City attacked by Cleon
22 Fabric with a raised pattern
23 Near ringer
24 "Jaws" locale
26 Canyon sound
28 Bring up
29 Work ___
31 Action star Steven
32 Blitz
33 Typing pool members
36 Designer Chanel
39 Make oneself heard in the din
43 Lecterns
45 "Tumbling Tumbleweeds" singer, 1935
47 Traveled far and wide
49 Eclipse shadow
51 Kind of splints
52 Butler's quarters?
53 Operatic prince
55 ". . . as a bug in ___"
56 Sally of NASA
59 Medic
60 Spanish gold
61 Timeworn
62 TV comic Louis

by Raymond Hamel

ACROSS

1 Guzzles
7 Bebop
11 Certain muscles, informally
14 Dislocate
15 Woodwind
16 Varnish resin
17 Ancient ascetic
18 Letter writing: Abbr.
19 Japanese admiral Yuko
20 Battleship
23 Mesmerized
27 "Or __!" (veiled threat)
28 "Torero Saluting" painter
29 Rioting
31 Despicable
32 Greek market
33 Mitigates
35 Actor Matheson or Allen
38 Dictionary
40 Rogers's partner
42 Wily
43 Topple
45 Fudd of cartoondom
46 Director's cry
47 Bee activity
49 __ Downs (English race track)
52 Contented sound
53 __ fixe
54 Bluff, with a gun
57 Nuclear defense grp.
58 Russia's __ Mountains
59 Slanted
64 Petition
65 Scoop (out)
66 To wit

67 "__! We Have No Bananas"
68 Whirlpool
69 Like Parmesan

DOWN

1 Neighbor of Ont.
2 Raises
3 "__ Gratis Artis" (MGM motto)
4 Enemy
5 Dear, as memories
6 Two-track
7 Oedipus' mother
8 Lodging
9 Swedish painter of "At the Granary Door"
10 "Fiddler on the Roof" star
11 Straighten

12 Wash up
13 "Waverley" novelist
21 Burstyn and Barkin
22 Labor org.
23 Iranian dollars
24 Theater backer
25 Stand-in
26 Actress Garr
30 Transistor predecessor
31 "__ Misérables"
34 Cronus, to Romans
35 Meek
36 "The woman" for Sherlock
37 Traffic sign
39 Choose
41 Prefix with meter
44 Just as much

46 Bill's partner
48 Vexing
49 Emerson piece
50 Aspect
51 Noted White House resident
52 Multicolored pattern
55 Slender nail
56 Sirius, e.g.
60 Drs.' org.
61 Tennis call
62 __ de France
63 Dancer Charisse

by Charles Arnold

34

ACROSS

1 Greatly impressed
5 Chairman ___
8 Poet Mandelstam
12 Charming
15 Viper
16 Moore of "A Few Good Men"
17 Sagan's "___ Brain"
18 40-Across's beloved 11
20 Shifty shoe?
22 African nation since 1993
23 Danger
25 Reps.
26 Close, as friends
29 Musician's job
31 Composer of "Socrate"
34 National park in Maine
36 Shem's father
38 Getting on
39 Indian writer Santha Rama ___
40 Theme of this puzzle
42 End up ahead
43 Frank Baum's initial initial
44 Angel's headgear
45 California's motto
47 Hebrew master
49 Dutch airline
51 Spinners, e.g.
52 Brain tests, for short
54 Essentials
56 Common speech
59 Bureau
63 Locale of 40-Across
65 Mourn
66 Prolific "author"
67 ___ pro nobis
68 Plains Indians
69 Items in a code
70 ___ Luthor
71 Boss Tweed lampooner

DOWN

1 Liturgical robes
2 Eroded
3 Bacchanalian cry
4 Crab, e.g.
5 Small rug
6 Late tennis great
7 It may be seria or buffa
8 Single-named folk singer
9 40-Across landmark
10 Hungary's Nagy
11 Galileo's home
13 40-Across's eastern border
14 Belgian river
19 Feature of 40-Across, according to Sandburg
21 Get-up
24 1860 nominee in 40-Across
26 Less cluttered
27 Florida city
28 1976 Nobel Prize winner from 40-Across
30 Indian district
32 "___ Ike" (50's slogan)
33 Millay and Ferber
35 Cry of discovery
37 Ripen
41 Kind
46 Type of roulette
48 Sets sail
50 Avg.
53 Pub perch
55 Therefore
56 Perfume holder
57 Humerus neighbor
58 Mary Robinson's land
60 Nintendo rival
61 Impending times
62 "Give it a ___"
64 Wailing instrument

by Christopher Hurt

ACROSS

1 Petite or jumbo
5 Gobs
9 Final Four rounds
14 Composer Satie
15 ___ avail
16 Gather into folds
17 Fashionable African land?
19 Chain of hills
20 Till compartment
21 Tartarus captive, in myth
22 Military encounter
25 ___ projection (map system)
27 Escargots
28 Embarassment
30 Accede (to)
31 Places of refuge
32 Neither's partner
34 "The Twilight of the ___"
35 Unites
36 Deal (out)
37 ___ Lanka
38 Birdie beater
39 "Give My Regards to Broadway" composer
40 Meeting musts
42 "Canterbury Tales" inn
43 Gabriel, e.g.
44 Curmudgeon-like
45 Composer Duparc
47 Courts
48 "___ Cowboy"
49 Fashionable state?
54 Enact
55 Zone
56 Arched recess

57 "Flowers for Algernon" author Daniel
58 ". . . leave no ___ unstoned"
59 Haydn's "Nelson," for one

DOWN

1 Wine description
2 George's lyricist brother
3 Address part
4 ___ out a living
5 Some temps
6 "Two Women" Oscar winner
7 Remnants
8 Tale of ___
9 Naiads' homes
10 Donizetti's "The ___ of Love"
11 Fashionable Canadian city?
12 "Othello" villain
13 Actress Anna
18 Curtain fabric
22 Silky-haired cat
23 Fashionable Welsh body of water?
24 Bonds
25 Scold
26 Rest on one's ___
27 Is weary
28 Summons
29 Person with a seal
31 Kind of tender
33 Rip
35 1977 Wimbledon champ
36 Crowds around

38 Turbojet and others
39 Movement
41 Infuriate
42 Paris or Hector
44 Cringe
45 Corn covering
46 Russian-born designer
47 "___ off to see . . ."
49 King Cole
50 Computer capacity, for short
51 Site of rejuvenation
52 Double twist
53 "You bet!"

by Joan Yanofsky

ACROSS

1 Yin's partner
5 Toy gun ammo
9 Rift
14 ___ patriae (patriotism)
15 Together, in music
16 "It ___ Be You"
17 Parisian entree
18 Old Vatican City monetary unit
19 Down Under soldier
20 1954 Hitchcock hit
23 Bonny one
24 Singer Acuff
25 Beautify
28 Barley bristle
30 Buddy
34 Spanish wave
35 Passage
37 Cain's nephew
38 Behave
42 Clam supper
43 Sacred song
44 Onetime medicinal herb
45 German donkey
46 Élan
47 Charitable foundations, e.g.
49 Chinese ideal
51 Part of a wagon train
52 Merit award
59 Use
60 Candy brand
61 Paint unskillfully
62 Mesa ___ National Park
63 Felipe, Jesus or Matty
64 Former Mormon chief ___ Taft Benson
65 Shipping amount

66 Desires
67 ___ Bien Phu (1954 battle site)

DOWN

1 Croquet locale
2 French call for help
3 ___ cloud in the sky
4 Edsel feature
5 Soft leather
6 Farewell
7 Result of tummy rubbing?
8 Ore layer
9 Maria Rosario Pilar Martinez
10 Jacks-of-all-trades
11 Wood trimmer
12 Weekly World News rival
13 Beaded shoe, for short
21 Chinese-Portuguese enclave
22 Coffee server
25 Ice cream mold
26 Biblical prophet
27 Thanks, in Thüringen
28 Journalist Joseph
29 Grieved
31 "My Dinner With ___"
32 Brimless hat
33 Test car maneuvers
36 18-wheeler
39 Iron pumper's pride
40 Diligent
41 Lagoon former

46 Actress Caldwell
48 Lacked
50 Locale in van Gogh paintings
51 Breakfast fruit
52 At any time
53 Betting game
54 Kind of vision
55 Fiddlers' king
56 "Schindler's List" extra
57 Fix
58 Israeli diplomat
59 Dow Jones fig.

by Arthur S. Verdesca

37

ACROSS

1 Good Queen ___
5 Paradisiacal spots
10 Interfraternity pres., e.g.
14 Latin 101 verb
15 On the up and up
16 ___ Major
17 Whopper maker
18 Delight
19 It gives skiers a lift
20 Clifton Webb film role
23 Carbon dater's calculation
24 Auto club letters
25 Amended
27 Suburbanite, perhaps
32 Seine feeder
33 Timetable abbr.
34 Delaware's capital
36 Cabinet post
39 Gulf War missile
41 Linda Blair in "The Exorcist"
43 Local theater
44 L'eggs rival
46 Wisconsin college
48 Mauna ___
49 "The More ___ You" (1945 song)
51 Toddler's transport
53 Côte d'Azur
56 One of the Three Stooges
57 Resident: Suffix
58 1971 Nitty Gritty Dirt Band song
64 Deuce or trey
66 Where vows are exchanged
67 Marshal Wyatt
68 Too
69 Aquarium fish
70 High gymnastic score
71 Da's opposite
72 Hopped out of bed
73 Stowe novel

DOWN

1 Wound soother
2 Abu Dhabi prince
3 Swedish auto
4 Gulf or jet follower
5 Grain ___
6 Proofreader's mark
7 "Holy moly!"
8 KNO₃
9 Sound system
10 On the other hand
11 Tom Selleck sports film
12 Kind of orange
13 Was concerned
21 Praise
22 Good's opponent
26 "This ___ outrage!"
27 The "C" in J. C. Penney
28 "Jaws" boat
29 Muscular moniker
30 In perpetuity
31 Kelly's co-host
35 Engrossed
37 Relative of the English horn
38 "Step to the ___"
40 Lucy's son
42 Oscar-winning Sally Field role
45 Look like
47 Shootout time
50 Book boo-boos
52 Map feature
53 Puerto ___
54 Land of Milan
55 More fit
59 Football Hall-of-Famer Graham
60 They preserve preserves
61 Hideout
62 Sea eagle
63 Made haste
65 Complete an "i"

by Gregory E. Paul

38

ACROSS

1 Israel's Dayan
6 Baby's bed
10 Attire for Dracula
14 Varsity starters
15 Frost
16 Plow animals
17 Comedy sketch with 29- and 44-Across
20 Pizza ingredient
21 Roseanne ___
22 Do art on glass
25 Luv
29 50's TV comedienne
32 Suspend
34 Oklahoma city
35 Fleur de ___
36 Choir voice
37 Election winners
38 Golden voiced Fitzgerald
39 "Agnus ___"
40 Yearly records
43 Kind of pad
44 50's TV comedian
47 Detail maps
48 Soot particle
49 ___ part (play on stage)
51 Envoy
56 Comedy sketch with 44-Across
61 "Do ___ others . . ."
62 DNA component
63 Bears places
64 Continue
65 Happy
66 Sgt. Bilko

DOWN

1 Cartoonist Groening
2 Roman emperor of A.D. 69
3 Appear
4 Mirthful reaction
5 Did B-grade stage work
6 Onetime Fidel ally
7 Circus stars Siegfried & ___
8 Metric foot
9 Expand
10 "Lord Jim" writer
11 Fireman's equipment
12 Apiece
13 U.S.C.G. officer
18 ___ Dame
19 Hill nymph
23 Giving up, as territory
24 Church songbooks
26 "First, You Cry" author Betty
27 "___ Survive" (disco hit)
28 Test format, often
29 Shenanigans
30 Italian actor Tognazzi
31 Islam adherent
32 31-Down who's been to Mecca
33 ". . . ___ and hungry look"
38 "Xanadu" rock group
40 Letter after gee
41 Money put aside
42 ___ Ste. Marie
45 Allen's "Annie Hall" co-star
46 Addison associate Richard
50 Genesis brother
52 Growl
53 Tennis score
54 Actress Copley
55 Gaelic
56 Wine container
57 Yoko ___
58 W.W. II area
59 Literary olio
60 Crimson

by David J. Kahn

ACROSS

1 6-Down finales
6 Corn waste
9 Conductor Riccardo
13 Ancient Greek marketplace
14 ___ polloi
15 Physically squelch
16 1. e4; e5
   2. Nf3; Nc6
   3. Bg5
19 Detective's assignment
20 Sugar suffix
21 Actor Estevez
22 Cousin of "Mayday!"
23 Cut in thirds
24 Neighbor of a knight
28 Name of 12 popes
29 "So long"
30 Stocking material
31 Debussy's had quite an afternoon
35 1. e4; c5
38 Frozen dew
39 Steelmaker's need
40 Property taxes in London
41 Lotto variant
42 Sherwood, e.g.
43 Doctorow best seller
47 Lose energy
48 Filmdom's May
49 Here, in Hyères
50 ___ even keel
54 1. e4; e5
   2. Nf3; Nc6
   3. Nc3; Nf6
57 Playwright William et al.

58 "___ is the winter . . ."
59 Wiser's companion
60 Kickoff props
61 Gun lobby inits.
62 Relative of 41-Across

DOWN

1 ___ Antony
2 Juárez water
3 Hellman's were in the attic
4 Gardner of mysteries
5 ___ Paulo
6 This puzzle's theme
7 Seep
8 Life story
9 Some skirts
10 Practical
11 Pick-me-up
12 Gold bar
15 Interstate haulers
17 One of the decks
18 Old-fashioned wig
22 Musical genre
23 Mark for mañana
24 Big party
25 Prefix meaning peculiar
26 Film director Vittorio De ___
27 One next in line
28 Suspiciously left, 50's style
30 France's ___ et-Loire department
31 Dread
32 First chips
33 Exploits
34 Place for eggs
36 Onetime refrigerant suppliers
37 Tadpole, eventually
41 Twists in a line
42 ___ accompli
43 Change the equipment
44 Solo
45 Pressure measurer
46 Michelins, e.g.
47 Unstressed vowel
49 Frankenstein's helper
50 Give the eye
51 Nothing, to a Nuyorican
52 The last word
53 Famed fiddler
55 Hotel
56 Weep

by Jay Livingston

40

ACROSS

1 Guinness or Baldwin
5 Old French coin
10 Resorts
14 Papal tribunal
15 Y's half brothers
16 Mr. Gingrich
17 Caesar's résumé?
20 Enters
21 Arrive feet first
22 Aunt ___ of "Oklahoma!"
24 Storm sirens
25 Former Clinton press secretary ___ Myers
28 It flows in the Ebro
30 New York's ___ Island
31 Geraint's wife
32 Passport endorsement
36 Fit
37 Century plant
38 Rock's Billy ___
39 Consider
40 Forum site
41 Bitter
42 Standard Oil logo
43 Barn sounds
44 Onetime phone company sobriquet
48 Russian ballet company
50 Moon-landing missions
52 Guard, e.g.
56 Cassius, to Caesar?
58 Turner of movies
59 Milton's "olive ___ of Academe"
60 Unwelcome roommate, perhaps
61 Barely makes, with "out"
62 Assistants
63 "___ for the poor"

DOWN

1 Bows
2 Boor
3 To be, to Bernadette
4 Advice from Caesar?
5 Easy
6 Get together, as grads
7 Pain
8 Entre ___
9 Graduation honors for Caesar?
10 Nasty
11 Pumpkin eater of rhyme
12 Expect
13 British guns
18 Man and Capri, e.g.
19 Handyman Bob
23 Went bananas
25 ___ ringer
26 North Sea feeder
27 Vogue rival
29 Award
31 Some are super
32 Caesar's opposite?
33 Think about it
34 Type
35 Priestly garb
37 Start of Caesar's comment at a museum?
41 "___ came a spider . . ."
42 Cockney greeting
43 Pickling solutions
44 Important Vermont tree
45 Approximately vertical, at sea
46 Carried
47 "___ Dream" ("Lohengrin" soliloquy)
49 "___ a Parade"
51 Asian dress
53 Shoppers' haven
54 Jot
55 Catches
57 Nonverbal affirmation

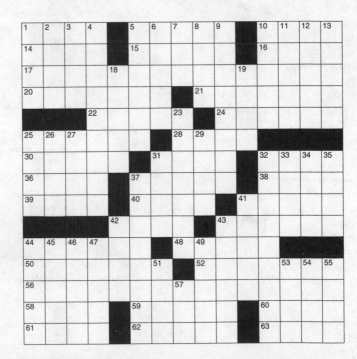

by Richard Hughes

ACROSS

1 Victim of Corday
6 Reminder
10 Kind of tongue
14 Wonderland lass
15 Graceful horse
16 Buy U.S. bonds
17 66-Across laurels
19 Bridge
20 Asserted
21 Wiped out in battle
23 Lover of sweets
24 Suffix with ballad or mountain
26 Wan
28 Taxi
31 Taste
33 Burlesque
36 Wings
38 Puppeteer Tony
40 Point of view
41 66-Across cry
44 Revolutionary War spy Major ___
45 First of all
46 Letters on a love letter
47 Peep show customers
49 Historic period
50 Napoleonic general
51 ___ Unis (United States, to Pierre)
53 Time Inc. workers
55 A Gershwin
57 Puppy bites
59 Acid salt
64 Cincinnati team
66 This puzzle's theme
68 Spoon-playing locale
69 One turn on an odometer
70 ___ operandi
71 Classify
72 Ripens
73 Trap

DOWN

1 Gullets
2 Landed
3 Actress Hayworth
4 Eight, to Hans und Franz
5 Titter
6 "___ overboard!"
7 Cupid
8 Miss Maples
9 Preoccupy the mind of
10 Silly one
11 66-Across garb
12 Ill-tempered czar
13 Car insurance case
18 Black Sea port
22 Plains harvest
25 Cowboy's rope
27 City south of Dallas
28 Chocolate source
29 Tag ___ with (accompany)
30 66-Across V.I.P.
32 Hardly a libertine
34 Arm bones
35 Vexatious
37 White heron
39 Hostile look
42 Broadcast again
43 Substance used to ignite firework fuses
48 Reputation harmer
52 Offshoot
54 Shuts with a bang
55 Irritates
56 City near Tahoe
58 Store event
60 Uniform collar
61 Verdi opera
62 Visitor's trip
63 Start of Massachusetts's motto
65 Collection
67 ___ Moines

by Sidney L. Robbins

42

ACROSS

1 "___ Breaky Heart"
5 Mavens
10 Apple of discord contender
14 Oxford, for one
15 Dickens's Heep
16 "___ calling"
17 Early TV western
20 State a new way
21 Near-homer
22 Hankers after
23 "Doggone it!"
25 Cessation
27 "Xanadu" band
28 Rose protector
29 Memory unit
30 Goes to sea
33 Former Attorney General Edwin
34 Flees after release
37 Substantive
40 Arm of the sea?
44 Queen and workers
45 In the future
47 ___ Tin Tin
48 Giant Mel
49 Tennis Hall-of-Famer Chris
50 "___ , the final frontier . . ."
52 Doctored
54 Newsman Arledge
55 Beginning
59 African snakes
60 Extremely cold
61 Luxuriant
62 ___ noire
63 Idyllic spots
64 Captain Hook's right hand, so to speak

DOWN

1 Cigarette tip
2 Bach work
3 Wish otherwise
4 Matzoh's lack
5 Underwater hazard marker
6 Vase
7 ___ Newtons
8 Ingredient
9 Former Israeli defense minister
10 Fastening device
11 Hex sign?
12 Mice, squirrels, etc.
13 At least one
18 ___ Vegas
19 Take a load off
22 Director Craven
23 Armada member
24 Gunfighter's wear
26 Scottish river
28 Mai ___
29 Mr. Lugosi
31 Ret. fleet
32 Word with light or write
33 Cal Tech rival
35 Pooped
36 Charades "little word"
37 Long March participant
38 Bubble over
39 Endeavor
41 A real head case?
42 Permit
43 Pilot's heading
45 Exact satisfaction for
46 Was noncommittal
49 Crimson rival
50 Soak (up)
51 Betting systems
53 Cathedral part
54 Country mail systems, for short
55 Poke
56 Flamenco cry
57 Five-spot
58 Charades "little word"

by Trip Payne

ACROSS

1 Twaddle
4 Obvious fact
10 Swiss peaks
14 Where Tel Aviv is: Abbr.
15 Illustrator Beardsley
16 Skin opening
17 Any ship
18 Brooklyn pitching legend
20 Ancient storyteller
22 Bowling alley button
23 Mass. senatorial monogram
24 ___ out (just managed)
26 Horned zoo animals, briefly
28 "Forrest Gump" author
33 Picnic pest
34 Dormitory disturbance
35 Capital of Bolivia
39 Super server, in tennis
41 Song syllables
43 Bridge feat
44 Chocolate substitute
46 Be of use
48 Belief
49 Subject of a 1956 film "search"
52 Overly rushed
55 Nose-in-the-air type
56 Moray
57 Jai alai basket
61 Take over
64 Former Idaho Senator
67 Pub quaff
68 Fork part
69 Major blood vessels
70 Howard or Ely
71 Safecracker
72 Fire stirrers
73 Sot's ailment

DOWN

1 Italian tower town
2 Court star Arthur
3 Awards show V.I.P.
4 Machine rods
5 Capek play
6 Over, to Otto
7 "Dies ___"
8 Parts of mins.
9 "You saved me!"
10 Showery mo.
11 Actress Sophia
12 Teaser ad
13 Hunts for
19 Group's tenets
21 Authorizes
25 Word of warning
27 Radio wise guy Don
28 W.W. II woman
29 Old-time Peruvian
30 Missile-warning grp.
31 Serious
32 Team track event
36 Coach's prop
37 Too hasty
38 TV prize
40 Gen. ___ E. Lee
42 Gets ready to fire
45 Building block
47 Expense account expenses
50 Polar cover
51 Milne's Baby ___
52 Packing a little weight
53 Creepy
54 Trolley sound
58 "Go away!"
59 Istanbul native
60 Commedia dell' ___
62 Cabal
63 Change for a twenty
65 Not pos.
66 Mercury or Saturn, e.g.

by Jon Delfin

44

ACROSS
1 Punchline reaction
5 Detective with a number one son
9 Dramatist Chekhov
14 Algerian seaport
15 Novelist Jaffe
16 "The Cloister and the Hearth" author
17 He's timely and reliable
20 Admits
21 Stream animals
22 "The shakes"
23 Troubles
24 Writer W. E. B.
28 Gielgud and Olivier, e.g.
29 Command to Fido
32 Woodwinds
33 Sicilian smoker
34 Bullring figure
35 He's friendly and party-loving
38 ". . . __ best friend"
39 Prong
40 Sam's sweetheart on "Cheers"
41 Gobbled
42 Regarding
43 Secured
44 __ bien
45 Spoil
46 Go at
49 Window type
54 He's versatile and adept
56 "A Lesson From __"
57 November word
58 Actress Lollobrigida
59 Paris subway
60 Pulitzer-winning author Herbert
61 Road for Caesar

DOWN
1 Popular roadside chain, for short
2 "Pretty Maids All in __"
3 Nuclear fission discoverer
4 Novelist Radcliffe and others
5 Horror movie locales
6 Says "to-whoo"
7 __ Domini
8 Turner or Cole
9 Mountain ridges
10 Tree houses
11 Record
12 Bouquet
13 New Jersey five
18 Not the modest sort
19 Cheer
23 Recoil
24 Belief
25 Ship sinker
26 Singer in white buck shoes
27 Multivolume dicts.
28 Shorthand user
29 Energy type
30 "Goodnight" girl of song
31 Trifled
33 Gives out
34 50-Down, e.g.
36 An end in __
37 One of 50-Down
42 Light musical piece
43 Maven
44 Selfish one
45 Island near Sicily
46 In __ (stuck)
47 Garage event
48 Burns, e.g.
49 Block
50 Christmas travelers?
51 Delete, with "out"
52 Hawaiian goose
53 Winter Palace resident
55 Actress Gardner

by Richard Hughes

ACROSS

1 Winter workers
10 Woodsy area
15 Place for the self-serving
16 Alternative to a Movado
17 Projects, in a way
18 Gulf of ___
19 Tint again
20 Group
22 ___ de plume
23 Hot time in Paris
24 What a commuter mustn't miss
27 Cuckoo
28 Underworld figures
30 Take a risk
31 Caramel-topped dessert
32 Disney pooch
34 Sad Sack's girlfriend, in the comics
35 Direct
40 ". . . ___ from our sponsor"
41 Wore
42 Miss out on a prize
43 Schiller's "___ Joy"
45 Fast fliers
49 Wolfed down
50 Some soon-to-be marrieds
52 Designate
53 ___ good turn
54 Samoan port, if repeated
55 Heavy clay
57 One-time Reagan co-star

59 Defunct women's magazine founded in 1989
62 Wing
63 "Sugar Babies" star
64 Frail
65 Like some tableware

DOWN

1 Went home
2 Must
3 "East ___"
4 To a high degree
5 Mertz or Merman
6 Grazing area
7 Directional suffix
8 Direct
9 Southwest Japanese port
10 Last year's srs.
11 He speaks: Lat. abbr.
12 "The Four Seasons" director
13 Cary Grant-like
14 Grilled
21 Part of a dog pound
25 Put ___ in one's ear
26 Dickens's Pecksniff
29 Replacement item
31 Babes in the woods
33 Pot top
34 Sign of success
35 Restaurant feature
36 Fairly solid, as odds
37 Emmy-winning comedienne
38 Lot
39 Repute

43 Spanish wave
44 Beliefs
46 Aussie tennis champ Fred
47 Turn the ___
48 Tridents
50 Sticky stuff
51 Vaccine developer
56 Secluded spot
58 British finale
60 Ribosomal ___
61 "___ Blue?" (1929 hit)

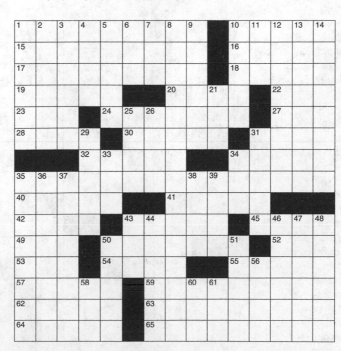

by David J. Kahn

ACROSS

1 Overfill
5 Attorney ___
10 Gulf of Aden vessel
14 Don of talk radio
15 ___-Dade County
16 Appian Way terminus
17 Trivial pests?
18 Jockey Cordero
19 Normandy river or department
20 Superlative suffix
21 Diminutive suffix
22 Nikita's successor
24 Nocturnal bird with an onomatopoeic name
27 Cottonseed product
28 "Like wow!"
32 Swedish toast
35 State of India
37 Baseball's Brock
38 "Mikado" refrain
42 Coach Parseghian
43 Mythical weeper
44 Salary
45 Arcade game
47 "Tea for ___" (1925 hit)
49 Chimera
55 Visit to the Serengeti
58 Trim
59 ___ es Salaam
60 All-comers' tournament
61 Cordial flavor
63 Skirt style
64 Carpal or physical beginning
65 Skate's cousin
66 ___-Rooter
67 Returnees from Reno, maybe
68 Keanu Reeves thriller
69 Lead

DOWN

1 Resilient strength
2 Lancaster County group
3 ___-frutti
4 Road twist
5 Explosive compound
6 Deep red Spanish wine
7 Pilsner
8 Soul: Fr.
9 Violent squall in the near-polar regions
10 Slobbers
11 ___ of plenty
12 Former Atlanta arena, with "The"
13 Pull dandelions, e.g.
21 Prefix with center
23 Fragrant resin
25 Pre-election product
26 Fritter away
29 ___ podrida
30 Synthesizer
31 30's chess champ Max
32 Trade
33 Dame ___ Te Kanawa
34 Paton of "Cry, the Beloved Country" fame
35 Bikini, e.g.
36 Bro. or sis.
39 Walking ___ (elated)
40 John of the Boston Pops
41 Former Polish city
46 Masters, in Africa
47 Filament
48 Small
50 Suppose
51 Savor
52 ___ savant
53 Sleigh driver
54 Before, with "to"
55 A few
56 Top
57 Gala
62 Forty winks
63 ___ Butterworth

by Christopher Page

ACROSS

1 Hubbub
4 Tray filler
7 "No, sirree!"
12 1972 Olympics star
16 In harmony
17 OPEC member
18 Man in red
19 "The Ferrari in the Bedroom" author
21 Start off
24 Doll's name
25 Appeal
26 Crossing word
27 Proven sound
30 Whiff
31 Dream team
36 "Heaven Must Have Sent You" singer
40 Unrigid
41 Barker
43 Track down
46 Upscale singer?
47 "Is it a boy __ girl?"
48 "Now I know why!"
51 Did with a passion?
53 West Coast Senator
57 Obscure
58 Charity
62 Jimmy Dorsey hit "Maria __"
63 Original Woodstock rocker
64 Synthetic fabric
65 From __ Z
66 TV actor Jack

DOWN

1 Bon follower
2 Baseball's Quisenberry
3 California fort
4 Grant portrayer
5 Canine command
6 Belonging to Li'l Abner
7 Lid fastener
8 Bonneville Flats site
9 Genuine
10 Not genuine
11 Chaired
13 Lollipop cop
14 "__ sad sight to see the year dying": FitzGerald
15 Newswoman Paula
20 Involve
21 Night shift worker
22 Ancient Dead Sea kingdom
23 Pro __ (like some legal work)
28 Ret. Atlantic flier
29 Atl. flier
31 Operating without __
32 One-dimensional
33 Set the pace
34 Bath bath
35 Book of the Apocrypha: Abbr.
37 Scottie Pippen's org.
38 Rephrase
39 Wander
42 Wander
43 Hurled, as grenades
44 By swallowing
45 List
46 Language of ancient Rhodes
49 Pilgrimage
50 Peek ending
51 On the money
52 Kind of ism
54 Curse
55 Sea east of the Caspian
56 Fit to serve
59 Accepts
60 Prefix with realism
61 Sign of popularity

by A. J. Santora

48

ACROSS

1 They rank above Pfc.'s
5 Address for a lady
9 Lamb servings
14 "Whoops"
15 "___ You" (Platters hit)
16 Protection
17 Metric prefix
18 Tetley products
19 Stag-party attendees
20 Many a Fifth Avenue habitué
23 Yevtushenko's "Babi ___"
24 ___ of March
25 Young faddist
30 Toy gun ammo
33 Overhead lighting?
34 Salt Lake City player
35 Lacking, with "of"
37 Hecklers' missiles
38 "Get lost!"
41 Drama award
42 Tsetses
44 Rhoda's mom, in 70's TV
45 Part of a paper roll
46 Countdown start
47 Nightclub gadabout
51 Role for Leontyne
52 Sloppy ___
53 Stovetop appliance
59 Life-jacket innards
60 Noodle
61 Commercial endorsement
63 Harsh
64 "Mystery" host Diana
65 Adm. Zumwalt
66 Snappish
67 Give ___ up (assist)
68 Engrossed

DOWN

1 Cow's chew
2 "That was close!"
3 Mathematical sets of points
4 Rudolph has one
5 Tourist transport
6 Once more
7 Voiced sigh
8 Gershwin-Weill ballad
9 Park patrons
10 Piles
11 Girl-watch
12 Fishing site
13 Draft org.
21 24 hours
22 Poem of praise
25 It's a steal
26 Two under par
27 Illinois city
28 How some stocks are sold: Abbr.
29 Jeopardy
30 Appear suddenly
31 Payola
32 Have the helm
36 It makes salsa picante
39 "Fables in Slang" author
40 Bridge alternative
43 Remain loyal to
48 Hubbub
49 Ms. Streisand
50 "Alley ___"
51 To the left, to Bligh
53 Stride
54 Unlocks, to Milton
55 Diamond of fame
56 Summon
57 Fitzgerald of scat
58 Roast cut
59 "Krazy ___"
62 Understood

by Lois Sidway

ACROSS

1 Prank
5 Brazilian dance
10 Trade
14 Needing irrigation
15 Actor Delon
16 "Oliver Twist has asked for ___!"
17 Marco Polo had it
19 Disconnect
20 Nautical sheet
21 Suffix
22 "Thar ___ blows!"
23 Crooked copy
25 Area for anchor cables
29 Vagrant
31 Somme's capital
33 Dubious
34 Tues. preceder
37 Dryer residue
38 Discombobulated
40 Soccer legend
41 Gave nourishment
42 Carrot, on occasion
43 Loewe collaborator
45 Of indeterminate gender
48 Liberate
49 Comes
51 Jar top
53 Like an old mattress
54 Maine's symbol
59 Rapier
60 Young genius
62 Legal writ, for short
63 Willow
64 Discontinued Dodge
65 Perceives
66 Actor George of "Cheers"
67 Board membership

DOWN

1 Scare film of '75
2 Smell ___ (detect wrongdoing)
3 ___ colada
4 Christian Scientist Mary Baker ___
5 Actress Bernhardt
6 On the same side, in war
7 Manhandle
8 Twice: Lat.
9 Aardvark morsel
10 Blur
11 Awe
12 Love
13 Big bloomer
18 German industrial city
21 Too stylish, perhaps
23 Colonial flute
24 Butcher's byproducts
25 ___ nelson
26 French friend
27 Oscar Wilde lady
28 Ready-go connector
30 Gone up
32 Tartar ___
35 Mr. Cassini
36 Imperious emperor
39 Very: Fr.
40 Early start
42 Latin literary lion
44 Respected tribesman
46 Lab measurers
47 Skipped over
49 Baldwin and Guinness
50 Calcutta coin
52 Like some gases
54 Nabokov novel
55 Some ring decisions
56 Frost
57 Central Sicilian city
58 Blue-pencil
60 "Hubba-hubba!"
61 "___ as directed"

by Christopher Page

50

ACROSS

1 Be sweet on
6 "Quiet!"
9 Boy Scout unit
14 The Bates ___, in "Psycho"
15 Soccer star Hamm
16 Baseball Hall-of-Famer Combs
17 Poolside wear
20 Flat formation
21 Harold Gray's Annie, for one
22 Louse-to-be
23 Mountain debris
25 Gate pivots
27 Bird of 29-Down
30 Smart-mouthed
32 Prefix with -asian
33 A, B, C, D or E
35 Marsh plant
39 Giveaway: Var.
41 Place for butts
43 Final authority
44 Copycat's words
46 Auction ending?
47 Race marker
49 Be a buttinsky
51 Disco flasher
54 Put a stop to
56 Jackie's second
57 Available, as a doctor
59 Org. for Annika Sorenstam
63 House wear
66 Kosher
67 Narc's grp.
68 Place for rouge
69 Idyllic places
70 Map rtes.
71 Acts the stool pigeon

DOWN

1 Radio letters
2 1996 Republican standard-bearer
3 Elevator maker
4 Meal
5 Polar helper
6 Campfire treat
7 Maximally cool
8 Truck stop fare
9 Court wear
10 "Awesome!"
11 Sumatra swinger
12 Pal of Kukla and Fran
13 Royal pains
18 Country singer Morgan
19 Contented sighs
24 Ranch wear
26 Russian's refusal
27 Gridiron "zebras"
28 Heavenly glow
29 Mouse, to a 27-Across
31 At the drop of ___
34 Audition tape
36 ___ Scott Decision
37 Celt or Highlander
38 Brontë's Jane
40 Hockey great Phil, familiarly
42 Mogadishu resident
45 Placed in a box, say
48 Late-night Jay
50 Oracle site
51 Fine fur
52 In a tough spot
53 Chain of hills
55 Fitzgerald and others
58 U.S.N. rank below Capt.
60 Hammer's end
61 Cyclist LeMond
62 Questions
64 ___ Tin Tin
65 I.B.M.-compatibles

by Kent Lorentzen

ACROSS

1 Lupino et al.
5 Rock band equipment
9 Swabs
13 "Cheers" habitué
14 French landscape painter
16 Toward shelter
17 Talk show host's holiday songs?
19 Holler
20 Interstice in a leaf
21 Goes first
23 Hog heaven?
24 County bordering London
25 Window frame
27 Actor's first course?
31 Wine cask
32 Swing around
33 Spitting ___
34 Education for the deaf
36 Carrot cousin
38 Street show
39 Bit of medicine
40 Car in a 1964 hit song
41 Artist's soup ingredients?
44 H.S. jr.'s exam
45 Tempestuous
46 Legal matter
47 Smart alec
50 Jesse James, e.g.
53 Buffalo's lake
54 Playwright's rubbish?
56 Drum sound
57 Moonshiner's need
58 Look ___ (explore)
59 Grandson of Adam

60 Old record company
61 Auspices: Var.

DOWN

1 "To Live and Die ___"
2 Active one
3 English composer's trap?
4 Unwrinkled
5 Clearasil target
6 Bossy's call
7 Musical intro
8 Sherry classification
9 Actress-director's vegetables?
10 Source of trans-fatty acids
11 Ill-gotten wealth

12 ___-serve (gas sign)
15 Russian kings
18 Foxy
22 Wish for
24 Poor part of town
25 Baby bird?
26 Ear-related
27 Capp and Capone
28 Film maker's argot?
29 Heebie-jeebies
30 Station
32 Mexican's nap
35 General's catch of the day?
36 Slow
37 Balaam's mount
39 Black mark

42 Lomond and Ness
43 Mistakes
44 "Dick Van Dyke Show" family name
46 Dull routine
47 "___ all in this together"
48 Press clothes
49 Cylindrical building
50 Norse capital
51 Italian wine center
52 "___ on first?"
55 R.N.'s skill

by Judith Perry

52

ACROSS

1 Arabian sultanate
5 Muddle
9 Insiders' talk
14 Take on
15 Word-of-mouth
16 Former Spanish P.M. ___ y Montaner
17 Semifictional movie
19 Circumvent
20 Alliances
21 One of the Huxtable kids
23 Increased, as inflation
27 ". . . on the Dead ___ Chest"
28 Like most music
29 Trounce
31 Photo repro
34 Plunders
36 The Emerald ___
38 Cider-sweet girl
39 "Metric" prefix
40 England-France connector
42 Witticism
43 Gender abbr.
44 Tedious undertaking
45 Much of Mali
47 Biblical beginning
49 Rounded ottoman
51 ___ Tots (grocery purchase)
52 Hold sway
54 Eulogists
56 Perry Como classic
59 B & B's
60 Hockey infraction
61 Mexican border language

66 Do detective work
67 Actress Garr
68 Lackawanna's railroad partner
69 Swiss mathematician
70 Good life
71 "Da Ya Think I'm ___ ?" (1979 hit)

DOWN

1 Unmatched
2 Chinese chairman
3 Trajectory
4 Sitting on the fence
5 Mushroom
6 Cleaned, as a disk

7 "Cheers" bartender
8 Eastern European
9 Frigidaire rival
10 Harsh-voiced birds
11 Number in the ball park?
12 Hockey's Bobby et al.
13 "See ya"
18 Local lingo
22 Moseys
23 Discord
24 On one's mark
25 Paid-for TV program
26 Bar request
30 Adm. or capt.'s org.
32 Worshiper

33 13th-century invaders
35 Circle and octagon, e.g.
37 Raising spirits
41 Road show grp.
46 Tribulations
48 Shade of meaning
50 Some mendicants
53 German gun
55 Gal with a gun, on Broadway
56 Fisherman's hope
57 Beige shade
58 Italian art patron
62 Spherical food
63 Wrath
64 Evening hour
65 "You there!"

by Wayne Robert Williams

53

ACROSS
1 Record player
5 Retrieve, as fly balls
9 Conclude successfully
14 The King's middle name
15 Deal (with)
16 Forgo
17 Bach's "___ in B Minor"
18 Place for Pete?
20 Part of a radio wave
22 Group of nine
23 Blockaded
24 One-liner
25 Fraternity letter
26 Kind of cue
28 Con artist's game
32 Thai money
34 "Easy Aces" medium
35 Rap's Salt-N-Pepa, e.g.
36 ___ Annie ("Oklahoma!" role)
37 Doing a takeoff
38 Canadian prov.
39 Upper cut?
41 Spirited
42 Regarding
43 "Dallas" actor Howard
44 Diner sign
45 "___ Doubtfire"
46 Ousted Ugandan
48 Argentine grasslands
51 Seasonal pick-me-up
54 90° arc
56 Place for Tyrone?
58 "___, Brute?"
59 Like some gases
60 Actress Merrill

61 A whole lot
62 Make the air fragrant
63 Call from the minaret
64 Unnamed ones

DOWN
1 Radical Mideast group
2 Shiraz native
3 Place for Jodie?
4 Discernment
5 Young haddock
6 Ruffian
7 Semicircular church section
8 $1000, slangily
9 Ritzy
10 Showing sincerity
11 Not on target
12 Part of the eye
13 Hang in the balance
19 Science course
21 Prefix with liberal
24 Nightclubs
26 Port Moresby resident
27 Pindar, e.g.
29 Place for Ben?
30 "___ We Got Fun?"
31 Marquand sleuth
32 Trunk cover
33 Direction for Solti
34 Andrew Johnson's birthplace
40 Carpentry machines

42 Antimacassar locale
45 Epithet for Anthony Wayne
47 Malory's "Le ___ d'Arthur"
48 Hymn of praise
49 Architectural piers
50 Book-lined room
51 Like Homer's "Illiad"
52 Missing
53 Verdon of "Red Head"
54 "Jeopardy!" is one
55 Annapolis inits.
57 Ladies' room, of a sort

by Bernice Gordon

54

ACROSS

1 Ingenuity
5 Vocational Identifiers
9 Singers Collins and Ochs
14 Roman emperor
15 Netman Arthur
16 Actress Taylor
17 1954 Gerard Philipe film
20 Guitar ridges
21 Pilot starter
22 Research room
23 Ogled
25 Had a lack
28 Worldwide lending org.
30 Yielding readily to pressure
32 Train freight holder
35 Clothes line
37 Malay boat
39 An Allman brother
40 1978 Ugo Tognazzi film
43 Coeur d' ___, Idaho
44 Bruins' school
45 Luce magazine
46 Irving Berlin's "All by ___"
48 Thundering group
50 Adversary
51 N.H.L. city
53 Change the decor
55 Lummox
57 Brothers, e.g.
59 Deck out
62 1974 Richard Kiley film
66 "The Hustler" author Walter
67 Cad
68 Pocket bread
69 Fuse, as ore
70 Catch sight of
71 Miss America prop

DOWN

1 "The Call of the Wild" animal
2 Roman way
3 1957 Joanne Woodward film with "The"
4 Black, as a chimney
5 Crone
6 On the briny
7 1987 Kevin Costner film
8 Siena seven
9 Start for fab or face
10 Biddy
11 1942 John Wayne film
12 "Star Wars" princess
13 Croat's neighbor
18 Functions
19 Leopold's partner in crime
24 Idiot
26 Idiot
27 Be jubilant
28 Mideast belief
29 ___-mouthed (insincere)
31 Lady of the haus
33 Wind: Prefix
34 Visit again
36 Artist Edouard
38 Car bar
41 Yiddish cash
42 "M*A*S*H" co-star Jamie
47 Eat not
49 "___ Diary"
52 Willow twig
54 Faucet problems
55 Mel and family
56 "Excuse me . . ."
58 Ooze
60 Exploits
61 Slangy okay
63 ___ Abner
64 Adherent's suffix
65 Thickness

by Wayne Robert Williams

ACROSS

1 Hair lines
6 Neeson of "Darkman"
10 Toe woe
14 Influence
15 Chills and fever
16 Margarine
17 Renowned cabaret crooner
19 Wee
20 Addison's literary partner
21 Marsh bird
23 Geese formation
24 Onetime Mideast inits.
26 Vacillates
28 Staircase adjunct
33 Water ___ ("Wind in the Willows" character)
34 Sandler of "Saturday Night Live"
35 Designer von Furstenberg
37 Gay city
41 Harry Kemelman sleuth
44 Flock of geese
45 Singer Horne
46 Blackhearted
47 Murphy, for one
49 Portray as satanic
51 Electrical units
55 123-45-6789, e.g.: Abbr.
56 "L'état c'est ___": Louis XIV
57 A little night music
59 More spooky
64 Bide ___ (stay a bit): Scot.
66 Vegas Impressionist

68 Epsilon follower
69 1994 film "___ Lies"
70 Magicians' props
71 Part of Q.E.D.
72 Actress Lamarr
73 "___ in the Dark"

DOWN

1 Cancer-causing compounds
2 "Thanks ___!"
3 After-shower wear
4 Toothpaste holder
5 Photograph needle
6 ___ di-dah
7 Lab assistant
8 Astral glows
9 Field of achievement
10 Folding 47-Across
11 Baseballer Tony
12 Extend a subscription
13 Poet Alfred
18 Like passengers during takeoff
22 Bounds
25 Fit for a king
27 Male flower part
28 Captain's insignia
29 Aleutian island
30 Local theater, to Variety
31 Drink
32 Wandered
36 Dressed to the ___
38 Sitarist Shankar

39 The Queen: Abbr.
40 Model Macpherson
42 Not moving
43 Distressed one?
48 Lack
50 New York lake
51 Stun
52 Lawn equipment
53 Michelangelo work
54 Steeple
58 Mideast missile
60 A.A.A. offerings
61 Longing
62 Nevada town
63 There's none for the weary
65 Dine
67 "Yoo-hoo!"

by Jon Delfin

56

ACROSS
1 Gymnast Korbut
5 Black
9 The "k" in 24k
14 "Where'er I ___
. . .": Goldsmith,
"The Traveller"
15 Family stories
16 Keep in stitches
17 Busy buzzer
19 Shakespearean
title role
20 Col. Klink's
domain, in
60's TV
21 Singer Anita
23 Sis's sib
24 Miss Gabor et al.
26 Alpine vocalist
28 Harry Blackmun
opinions, often
32 Cattle
33 Balderdash
34 Language
of Dundee
36 Music with
a beat
39 Reuniongoer,
informally
41 Standing up
43 Not working,
as a battery
44 Street urchin
46 Bogged down
48 Mimic
49 ___ Bones
(Ichabod
Crane's rival)
51 Melville's
Ishmael, e.g.
53 Dieter's worry
56 Bluenose
57 "The loneliest
number"
58 Gymnastic
equipment
60 Maltreat
64 Shinbone

66 Dish for
the deflated
68 Take ___ for
the worse
69 Not written
70 ___ end
(stopped)
71 Onomastics study
72 Erotic
73 Pops' partners

DOWN
1 Eyeballs
2 Boor
3 Vasco da ___
4 Strolls
5 Poshness
6 TV's Newhart
7 Item dunked
in milk
8 In want
9 Singing insect

10 Maupassant's
"Bel ___"
11 Model A feature
12 Stick out like
___ thumb
13 Canio, e.g.,
in "Pagliacci"
18 Washes
22 Hunky-dory
25 Nor'wester
27 Geraint's
beloved
28 Long puff
29 Southeast
Kansas town
30 Lummox
31 Oktoberfest
vessel
35 Throw away
37 Mafia kingpin
38 Wroclaw's river
40 Painter Joan

42 Quite, to
the British
45 Conquerors
of 1066
47 Boot camp
routine
50 "Mamma ___!"
52 Shining
53 Trig function
54 Santa ___ race
track
55 Group character
59 Slangy yes
61 ___ no good
62 Famous twins'
home
63 Nighttimes,
in poetry
65 Fury
67 Nth degree

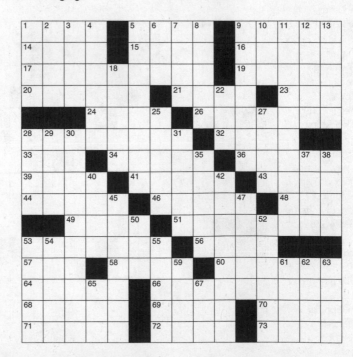

by Robert R. Zimmerman

ACROSS

1 B followers
4 Philippine island
9 Writer LeShan
12 Penned
14 Thin pancake
15 Campaign donor, for short
16 Have airs, like Rover?
18 Dockers' org.
19 Gleaming
20 Shady
22 Washington's Mount St. ___
24 Director Fred et al.
25 Have it rough, like Asta?
30 "___ make myself clear?"
32 Hockey feint
33 Art school subj.
34 Author Ferber
36 Transplant
39 Goods: Abbr.
40 Sleeps in a sitting position
41 Spanish other
43 Tom Jones's "___ Not Unusual"
44 Get Marmaduke's reaction?
49 Rock's ___ Straits
50 Clothes
52 Patron of France
55 Remedial workshop
57 Inventor's cry
58 Visit the pound?
61 Dickens pen name
62 "Oklahoma!" aunt
63 Relaxing bath
64 Afore
65 Plow man
66 180° from NNW

DOWN

1 Teen love
2 Jitterbug
3 Prima ballerina
4 Acad. or univ.
5 "___ you for real?"
6 Doc
7 Moral fable: Var.
8 Sliding door grooves
9 Of great size
10 Mustachioed artist
11 "___ may look on a king"
12 F.D.R. program
13 Group of nine
17 Proffer
21 Ali's faith
23 Benefit
26 Station
27 Native
28 Eschew food
29 Hot times in Saint-Tropez
30 Fender bender
31 Skunk's defense
35 Stage mutter
37 Will'___'wisp
38 Soldier's line of defense
42 Discombobulates
45 Imparted a slight taste to
46 Baltimore bird
47 Get cozy
48 "A Dog of Flanders" author et al.
51 Actress ___ Hasso
52 Kemo ___ (trusty scout)
53 Air Force missile
54 Flabbergast
56 Inits. for R. E. Lee
59 "___ the ramparts . . ."
60 Uno + due

by Ernie Furtado

58

ACROSS
1 Vacuum tube filler
6 Wanders
11 Underwear initials
14 March composer
15 Key above G
16 Majors or Myles
17 Happenchance
19 Once __ while
20 Barber of baseball
21 Sprite
22 Made
24 City near Utah Lake
26 "Desire Under the __"
29 Head of a familia
30 Peeved
33 When Operation Overlord took place
34 Bygone coif
36 Mmes., across the Pyrenees
38 Dined
39 Jodie Foster's directorial debut, 1991
43 Douglas or alpine, e.g.
44 Choir members
45 Pub quaffs
46 Seventh day activity
48 Improves
51 Monkeyshine
53 Carriage, in the country
54 Cousin of the English horn
58 Bushy-tailed animal
60 Princess's sleep disturber
62 Dishcloth
63 Greek vowel
64 Child's means of propulsion
68 Soak flax
69 More cheerful
70 Takes to the trails
71 Opposite NNW
72 Brainstorms
73 Apply

DOWN
1 Houston player
2 Oarsman
3 Tour leader
4 W.W. II Intelligence org.
5 N.B.A.'s Archibald
6 Club fund-raiser
7 Light switch position
8 Miss. neighbor
9 Chess finale
10 Robert Fulton's power
11 Notoriously risky social event
12 Respects
13 Sharpshooter
18 Fashion's Cassini
23 "Far out"
25 Shopping place
27 1939 James Stewart title role
28 Que follower, in song
31 __ bene
32 Mr. Quayle
34 Drives away
35 A-number-1
37 Christmas tree topper
40 Atty.'s degree
41 Parisian summers
42 What's more
43 Constitution creators
47 Actor Matheson
49 Narrows
50 Watchful one
52 Welsh dog
55 Accelerator's counterpart
56 Western
57 Cast out
59 Little hopper
61 North Carolina county
65 Drain cleaner
66 Pasture
67 General Mills cereal

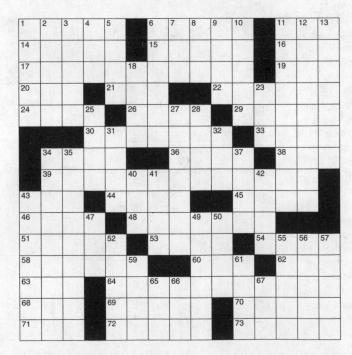

by Rich Norris

ACROSS

1 Wasn't colorfast
4 "Le ___ de Monte Cristo"
9 Napoleon's force
14 Gardner of "Mogambo"
15 1935 Triple Crown winner
16 Closes in on
17 Coastal area
19 Birdlike
20 Unyielding
21 Driver's need
23 Old town official
25 Gets the soap out
26 Investigated with "about"
29 No-caffeine drink
31 Drives
33 Freight weight
34 Part of Q.E.D.
37 ___ capita
38 Had a hankering
41 Anger
42 Barber's action
44 Stars and Bars inits
45 Commandment breaker
47 Batman, to the Joker
50 Astronomer Carl
51 "___ and rejoice": Psalms
53 Under, in verse
55 Largest newspaper in Calif.
57 Became less clear
61 Chilean port
62 Major pipe
64 Family car
65 "Hard ___ I" (nautical command)
66 Mr. Gershwin
67 Idyllic spots
68 Legal wrongs
69 "___ Miz"

DOWN

1 Pro ___
2 Eager
3 Zilch, to Zapata
4 Like Lahr's lion
5 Mideasterner
6 Dull finishes
7 Word before more and merrier
8 Jazzman Hines
9 Tylenol alternative
10 Income
11 Watch's center
12 Clear the slate
13 Workers of puzzledom
18 Host
22 Worth and Castle
24 Give new job skills
26 Small drinks
27 Augury
28 Full moon occurrence
30 "___ Ryan's Express"
32 Leave the union
35 Space
36 Slender-billed sea bird
39 Palm Sunday mount
40 Warps
43 Big-billed sea bird
46 Biblical prophet
48 Marseille moms
49 Pie slice, in geometry
51 World-weary
52 Like many seals
54 On the qui vive
56 The Sultan of ___
58 Dublin legislature
59 Dublin's country
60 Genetic materials
63 G.I.'s address

by Christopher Page

60

ACROSS

1 Snitch
6 1986 World Series champs
10 "You said it!"
14 More washed out
15 Over
16 Pop singer Laura
17 Senator Specter
18 Pro __
19 Bushy hairstyle
20 1970 George Harrison hit
23 Astronaut's "fine"
24 Catch sight of
25 Tropical animals
27 Bill Haley's band
30 Tackle box gizmo
32 Jazz's Kid
33 Stendhal hero Julien
35 Wedding guest
38 Take à la magicians
40 Sinatra standard
42 Wise
43 February forecast
45 Katmandu's land
47 Narcs' grp.
48 "So Big" author
50 Robert Shapiro, e.g.
52 Singer West
54 Pocket bread
55 Shoemaker's helper, in story
56 60's sitcom
62 Composer Janacek
64 Nabisco brand
65 Walkie-talkie
66 Landlocked Asian country
67 Void's partner
68 In __ (stuck)

69 Scurriers
70 Strike out, as copy
71 Post offices have them

DOWN

1 W.W. II meat
2 On one's guard
3 Woes
4 Shortstop Reese
5 Hemingway and others
6 "Back to the Future" role
7 List shortener
8 Baum dog
9 "In the Heat of the Night" locale
10 Literary olio
11 Lerner-Loewe musical
12 Inaccuracy
13 Crannies
21 British college
22 "Tuna-Fishing" painter
26 Bic products
27 Flatfoots
28 Ph.D. exam
29 1989 Daniel Day-Lewis film
30 Underground way
31 Applaud
34 Sandberg of the Cubs
36 "The African Queen" screenwriter
37 Abrade
39 Track contest
41 Ivy Leaguer
44 Barbershop request
46 Football fling
49 __ question (certainly)
51 Japanese mustard
52 Perry's secretary
53 City SSE of Buffalo
54 Capitalist tool
57 Quiz choice
58 Terrible rigor
59 Norse chief
60 Supreme Court complement
61 Lays down the lawn
63 Draft letters

by Gregory E. Paul

61

ACROSS

1 Blvd. crossers
4 #2, informally
8 Defeater
 of Hannibal
 at Zama
14 Pasture
15 Shakespearean
 villain
16 Chaucer's ___ Inn
17 Civil war, e.g.
19 List ender
20 Mr. Rathbone
21 Dour
23 Chicago-to-
 Atlanta dir.
24 Slept "soundly"
26 "Hud" Oscar
 winner Patricia
28 Snap, crackle
 and pop, e.g.
34 Criminal charge
37 City on
 the Mosel
38 Razor sharpener
39 Help in the
 getaway
41 Architectural
 piers
43 Location
44 Catcalls
46 Moffo and
 Magnani
48 In low spirits
49 Fe, fi, fo,
 fum, e.g.
52 Willing
53 Swimwear
 manufacturer
57 Perform
60 Pole figure
63 Be unfaithful to
64 "Calm down!"
66 "Life is a bowl
 of cherries," e.g.
68 White winter
 coat
69 Primary

70 More than none
71 Clears of hidden
 problems
72 Rival rival
73 Born

DOWN

1 Neatniks'
 opposites
2 Ross Perot, e.g.
3 Final authority
4 Cataclysmic
5 Attention
6 Sometimes
 they're super
7 ___ l'Évèque
 (French cheese)
8 Not monoaural
9 Dozes
10 Olympic
 basketball
 coach Hank

11 Buddies
12 Rainbow goddess
13 Garfield's foil
18 Spanish
 Surrealist
22 One in the
 running
25 "Dumb ___"
 (old comic)
27 Plenty
29 Mosque feature
30 Big name in
 insurance
31 Goddess
 of discord
32 Least bit
33 Mimicked
34 Indian prince
35 Victim of sibling
 rivalry
36 Sir Robert of
 London's bobbies

40 Advanced math
42 "Je ne ___ quoi"
45 Averring
47 Elsa in
 "Lohengrin"
50 Overacts
51 ___ tide
54 Wharton's Frome
55 Lorna of an
 1869 romance
56 Deli phrase
57 Scored a
 hole-in-one
58 Inner workings
59 Grave
61 Poet Lazarus
62 More than a snack
65 N.Y. school
67 Waitress's bit

by Richard Hughes

ACROSS

1 Scenic view
6 Hombres' homes
11 E.T.S. offering
14 Back way
15 "Yup"
16 Four-in-hand
17 John ___
19 Military inits.
20 Kind of diet
21 Tango requirement
22 Cob or drake, e.g.
23 Well-groomed
25 Red wine
27 ___ Mahal
30 Wineglass part
32 Right: Prefix
33 Sharif and Bradley
35 Mr. Fixit
39 Backgammon equipment
40 Attribute
41 River of northern France
42 Sure thing?
44 Mooring site
45 Exposed
46 Campus building
48 ___ Palmas, Spain
49 Guiding light
51 Logs some z's
53 Log some z's
54 Auditor, for short
57 Arabian coffees
61 Skill
62 John ___
64 Half of a 1955 merger
65 Serf
66 Garden bulb
67 At any time, poetically
68 British ___
69 Musial and Laurel

DOWN

1 Like fireplace logs
2 Advertising award
3 "___ right with the world"
4 Relative of the weasel
5 Huxley's "___ in Gaza"
6 Wrigley Field player
7 "Cat on ___ . . ."
8 Third place
9 Overlord
10 "Listen!"
11 John ___
12 Bride's path
13 Bit of dogma
18 Immediately, in the operating room
22 Diacritical mark
24 ___ firma
26 Garland
27 One of Taylor's exes
28 Friend of François
29 John ___
31 1971 hit "___ Bobby McGee"
34 Edit
36 Mountaineer's spike
37 Voyaging
38 Seines
40 Infantry lines
43 Spanish treasure
44 Customs duties
47 Incline
49 Drill grip
50 Halloweenlike
52 Advance person
55 Medicinal tablet
56 Medicinal plant
58 Hawaiian dance
59 "Z ___ zebra"
60 Weakens
62 Upsilon's successor
63 "___ De-Lovely"

by Albert J. Klaus

ACROSS

1 Kind of acid
6 ___ de Triomphe
9 Doesn't read carefully
14 Another kind of acid
15 Mousse alternative
16 Apportion
17 Santa Clara Co. address
19 Lose one's amateur status
20 Affront
21 ___ Speedwagon
23 Finsteraarhorn is one
24 Property restriction
25 Bowling alley buttons
28 Bobby here
29 Draft org.
30 Obsess
31 Flimflam
32 Carnation spot
33 Less 32-Down
34 Author of 2005's "Juiced"
37 Political pamphlet
39 Skylark maker
40 City near Sparks
41 Tutu event
43 Summit
46 Summer drink
47 "Rabbit Run" and "Rabbit Redux," e.g.
48 "___ Lisa"
49 Colorado Indian
50 Be in the red
51 Bullet type
53 "A Year in Provence" author Peter
55 "Forget it!"
58 Shower time
59 In high spirits
60 Cicero's was Tullius
61 Oozes
62 Make a palindromic living?
63 Upright

DOWN

1 Two Byzantine emperors
2 Some Mideasterners
3 Gets the soap out
4 ___ Joe, of "Tom Sawyer"
5 Refrigerate
6 Census info
7 Room type
8 Bordeaux, e.g.
9 Nigeria's former capital
10 Jeff Lynne rock band
11 "The Godfather" actor
12 "A Chorus Line" song "What I Did ___"
13 Cork in a bottle
18 Zebra feature
22 Summer on the Seine
26 Bigwig
27 Having a market, as goods
30 Speedy
31 Part of a royal flush
32 Batty
33 Splinter group
34 Brontë heroine
35 Void's partner
36 Bedtime for Alonzo
37 Psychological injuries
38 Bureaucracy
41 Theatrical finale
42 Settle a score
43 Still ahead
44 "Hold on"
45 Company with a subsidiary
47 Christmas songs
48 Word before league or domo
52 Sandberg of baseball
54 Back talk
56 Maryland's state tree
57 Three-way circuit

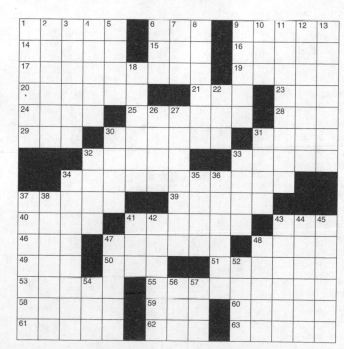

by Matt Gaffney

64

ACROSS

1 Keep ___ (persevere)
5 Sitcom diner
9 Most of Iberia
14 Dial sound
15 In ___ (mired)
16 Glue
17 Goldwyn discovery Anna ___
18 Houston university
19 Get the lead out
20 Geology, e.g.
23 Gibson of tennis
24 Three, in Thuringen
25 Sheepcote comment
28 Baseball's Maglie
29 ___ rod (Biblical item)
31 Airborne particulates
34 Where Lois and Clark work
38 Hook's henchman
40 River, in 9-Across
41 "American Gigolo" actor
42 Athlete's ambition
47 Pitch
48 Post-W.W. II Prime Minister
49 Golfer Woosnam
51 ___ Perce Indians
52 Imitated
55 High points
59 Shakespearean showplace
61 Cousteau concern
64 Pivot
65 Follow
66 Slick vehicle?
67 Seasons on the Somme

68 Gen. Robt. ___
69 Annual tournaments
70 Tweed Ring lampooner
71 Monster's loch

DOWN

1 On the briny
2 Utter
3 Like argon
4 Nine ___ of the law
5 Sicilian port
6 Idle of "Monty Python"
7 Clear
8 Guide
9 Regular programming pre-emptor
10 Peel

11 Naked ___ jaybird
12 1986 hit "___ Only Love"
13 Born
21 Kind of waiter or water
22 Tide type
25 Noted Seine landscapist
26 End of ___
27 Late bloomer
30 Old barroom tune
31 City on the Nile
32 Slew
33 Airport booth leaser
35 Anger
36 Permit: Abbr.
37 "___ hoo!"
39 Pipe connection

43 From whom buyers buy
44 Cult film "___ Man"
45 Superlatively wealthy
46 The brave do it
50 Tidy up
53 Buddy of TV
54 Actress Burke
56 Out-of-date
57 Hears, as a case
58 Graf rival
59 Secluded valley
60 Calendar abbr.
61 Court
62 Start of a cheer
63 Pub brew

by Randy Sowell

ACROSS

1 "Lights out" tune
5 U.S. terr. until 1912
9 Dieter's lunch
14 Opposite of sans
15 ___ Raton
16 Noted violinmaker
17 Chaucer's Wife of ___
18 Radar screen image
19 Kayak
20 Pre-Utah team
23 Breakfast-in-bed item
24 Comic Johnson
25 Put on years
26 Hushed
28 Priest's robe
30 Clairvoyance
33 Alcohol awareness org.
35 Writer Fleming
37 Slender
39 Pre-Los Angeles team
42 Elicited
43 Anglo-Saxon letter
44 "Typee" sequel
45 Like Gen. Powell
46 Dadaist Hans
48 Ukr. or Russ., once
50 Some dash widths
51 Eurasia's ___ Mountains
53 King ___
55 Pre-Indianapolis team
61 Furnish
62 Artful
63 Manhandle

65 American Kennel Club rejects
66 Sister and wife of Osiris
67 New York canal
68 Mississippi tributary
69 Mammilla
70 Cell: Prefix

DOWN

1 Bill
2 Trendsetting, perhaps
3 Waned
4 ə
5 This ans., e.g.
6 Kind of bed
7 Colder
8 Revolutionary Emiliano
9 Pouches
10 Key of Mozart's Symph. No. 29
11 Actress Turner
12 The gamut
13 Number after nueve
21 Olive that's very thin
22 TV family, 1952–66
25 Jurassic Park compound
27 Crude container
29 Brief letters?
30 Basic
31 Forte
32 Mexican moola
34 Happy associate
36 Opposite SSE
38 I, to Claudius

40 Mauna ___
41 Reading problem?
47 Loss's partner
49 Orson Welles studio
52 Stood up
54 Early Mexican
55 The Ronettes' "___ Baby"
56 Shade of blue
57 Jump for Oksana Baiul
58 One of the Jackson 5
59 ___ facto
60 Skin abnormality
64 Pope who excommunicated Martin Luther

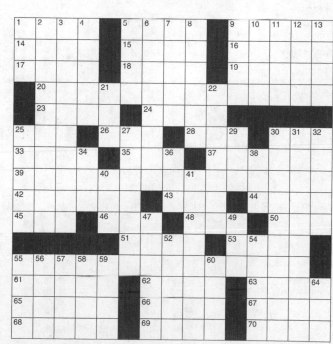

by Martin Schneider

66

ACROSS

1 Naïve ones
6 Crosswise to a ship's middle
11 ___ Malaprop (Sheridan character)
14 Massey of "Love Happy"
15 Yankee Yogi
16 Hour on a grandfather clock
17 Twiggy broom
18 End-all's companion
19 One-liner
20 "Unfinished"
23 "Glitter and Be ___" ("Candide" song)
24 Coop denizen
25 State of France
26 Relieved sound
29 "Foucault's Pendulum" author
31 "Ich bin ___ Berliner"
33 Lennon's lady
34 Crack the case
36 More pleasant
40 "Classical"
43 Reddish dye
44 ". . . and ___ grow on"
45 Ingested
46 Approves
48 ___ Lanka
49 Home of Iowa State
50 Severe disappointment
53 Overhead rails
55 Hokum
57 "Kaddish"
63 Great many
64 Coordination loss: Var.

65 Pavarotti, for one
66 Prefix with sex or cycle
67 Beau ___
68 Mother's-side relative
69 Aerialist's safeguard
70 Clockmaker Thomas et al.
71 M.P.A.A. approved

DOWN

1 Lobster eaters' needs
2 British P.M. Douglas-Home
3 Hokum
4 Ample
5 Dance in Rio
6 A.M. or P.M., e.g.
7 "Pastoral"
8 Remove chalk
9 Francis of "What's My Line"
10 Neighbor of Senegal
11 Strength
12 Cowboy's rope
13 Tourist attraction
21 Ken Follett's "___ the Needle"
22 Bottled spirits
26 Undergrad
27 Apropos of
28 Thug
30 Sister of Euterpe
32 Dope
34 Good, long bath
35 Always
37 Study for finals
38 Villa-building family

39 Hwy. numbers
41 Understood
42 Swizzles
47 Certain sofa
49 Parthenon goddess
50 Kid's shooter
51 Sierra ___
52 Trip that's out of this world?
54 Slightest
56 Aquatic mammal
58 Loses rigidity
59 Actress Carrie et al.
60 ___ the kill
61 Learning method
62 1857's ___ Scott Decision

by Nancy S. Ross

ACROSS

1 Witches
5 "The Metamorphosis" author
10 Office honcho
14 Skin soother
15 Violas' neighbors in an orchestra
16 It's west of Ark.
17 "Love ___ leave it"
18 "Hungry Like the Wolf" singers
20 Vegetarian's no-no
22 Twixt 12 and 20
23 Actor Dick of "Bewitched"
24 Defense acronym
25 ___ cum laude
27 Freight weight
28 Poet laureate Cecil Day ___
32 Juárez ones
33 Remove vital parts from
34 Scold
35 6 on a phone
36 Bullfighter
38 Actor Cariou
39 San Diego nine
41 Panhandle
42 Fakir's income
43 More cagey
44 "Kidnapped" monogram
45 Eliminate
46 See eye to eye
48 Defect
49 They're far out
52 Candy from a machine
55 1969 hit by the Archies
57 Mr. Nastase

58 Counterfeiters' foes
59 Muslim prince
60 Hawkeye Pierce's portrayer
61 Dian Fossey subjects
62 British tube
63 "A bit of talcum/is always walcum" writer

DOWN

1 Tresses
2 Der ___ (Adenauer)
3 Self-righteous
4 O'Hara's "___ and Soda Water"
5 Minolta rival
6 Adjoin
7 Part of F.Y.I.

8 1977 Oscar actress
9 Six-time Emmy winner Ed
10 Rascal
11 Green pods
12 Dross
13 Mentally sound
19 Casino employee
21 Victorian, for one
24 Distinguished
25 Parotitis
26 Historical record
27 Howard Carter's 1922 discovery
29 Whitman College site
30 Paraphernalia
31 Taste or touch
33 Oil alternative

34 Swamp
36 Wall Street news
37 TV host O'Connor
40 Former White House family
42 Kind of coffee
44 Job hunter's need
45 Slippery ___
47 Calibrate anew
48 Like winter animals
49 Hammett hound
50 Low-cut shoe
51 Double curve
52 Food critic Greene
53 Pots' tops
54 Wife of Jacob
56 Toothpaste type

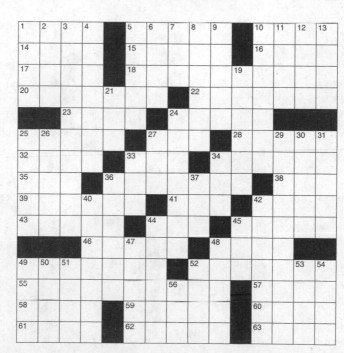

by Gregory E. Paul

ACROSS

1 Practical jokes
5 School founded by Henry VI
9 Sharp-smelling
14 For men __ (stag)
15 "Kon-Tiki" craft
16 Haunted house noises
17 They're easily bruised
18 The __ of the party
19 Leaning slightly, as a ship
20 Passenger restraints
22 Sudden shock
23 Change, as a hem
24 Paramount workplace
25 Path of Discovery
27 Island near Australia
29 White weasel
30 Followed tenaciously
32 Rainbows
33 Last mile in a car warranty, often
38 University founder Cornell
39 Shops
40 Be that as it may
42 Painstaking
47 TV host Gibbons
48 Cleopatra's biter
49 Artoo-__
50 Gottfried, in "Lohengrin"
51 Tour outline
53 Tour of duty
54 Nil, in Seville
55 Chorister
56 Eyelashes
57 Spanish crowd?
58 Haymarket Square event
59 Football's Papa Bear
60 "__ Grand Night for Singing"
61 Comic Carvey

DOWN

1 Attacks
2 Actress Lansbury
3 Is a bad winner
4 Word with solar or nervous
5 __ Stanley Gardner
6 Firefly component?
7 Leading early in the race
8 Military experiment, perhaps
9 Key of Beethoven's Seventh
10 Play-by-play announcer's partner
11 Front-row racing fan
12 1992 thriller "Basic __"
13 Aug. clock setting
21 Diamond Jim
26 New age musician John
28 "__ fast, buster!"
29 Car bomb?
31 "Medea" playwright
33 "I __ Fine" (Beatles hit)
34 Russian newspaper
35 Voluntary capacity
36 Dar es Salaam's land
37 Stage comment
41 Christmas bell ringers
43 Actor Depardieu
44 It may be last on the list
45 Boxer Ken
46 Corolla, e.g.
48 "__ a stinker?": Bugs Bunny
52 Cape Canaveral acronym
53 Univ., e.g.

by Bob Klahn

69

ACROSS
1 Beat, as wings
5 Biblical symbol of patience
8 Spain's Bay of __
14 Civil rights figure Parks
15 Unlatch, poetically
16 Skewer
17 "__ Breaky Heart"
18 Still, to Steele
19 Short stops
20 Intense interrogation
23 International traveler's need
24 Norse chief
25 Artery clogger
28 Pirate's sword
30 Lived
33 Lover of Narcissus
35 Albee's "The __ Story"
36 Romeo's rendezvous
38 Journalists, collectively
42 Ionian island
43 __ with (tease)
44 To be, in Paris
45 Clod buster
46 Picked up the dinner tab
50 Gyroscope's cousin
51 Counterfeit coin
52 Stairway component
54 Refusing to testify
60 Minor task
61 Old World deer
62 __ vision (Superman skill)
63 Prattle
64 30's home run king

65 See 30-Down
66 Fast
67 Like: Suffix
68 Guitar's ancestor

DOWN
1 Sigma Chi, e.g.
2 __ Ness
3 Ace-serving Arthur
4 Programs for purchase
5 Mendacious salesman of old car ads
6 0 on a telephone
7 River curve
8 They stand on their own two feet
9 Ezra Pound and Amy Lowell, e.g.

10 Reject with disdain
11 Four six-packs
12 Away from the weather
13 Oui or ja
21 Here: Lat.
22 __ good turn
25 Go get
26 Sneeze sound
27 When repeated, a comforting phrase
29 1970 hit "Whole __ Love"
30 With 65-Across, Dodge City lawman
31 Houston player
32 Brew in a teapot
34 Not working
37 Rd. or hwy.

39 Summarized
40 Flamboyant successes
41 Upper canines
47 Become depleted of water
48 Omelet need
49 Rock's __ Leppard
51 Slide on ice
53 Computer dot
54 Catch animals
55 "Verrrrry interesting" Johnson
56 "Star Trek" counselor
57 Haus wife
58 Small pastry
59 Preposterous publicity
60 Nav. rank

by Harvey Estes

70

ACROSS

1 Bongo or conga
5 Bellhop's burden
8 Integra maker
13 Diarist Frank
14 Concert halls
16 "Vacancy" sign site
17 Star of 59-Across
20 Got 100 on
21 Extinct bird
22 Brazilian hot spot
23 Director of 59-Across
27 Pampering, briefly
28 Olive ___
29 Saragossa's river
30 Circusgoers' sounds
32 Understand
34 "___ Irish Rose"
38 Music featured in 59-Across
42 English assignment
43 Slangy refusal
44 Classic soda brand
45 Tiff
48 PBS funder
50 III, to Jr.
51 Author of 59-Across
56 A.F.L. merger partner
57 Suffix with Peking
58 "___ #1!"
59 Theme of this puzzle, with "A"
65 Like bell-bottoms, nowadays
66 Claudius's successor
67 Highlander
68 Bus. aides
69 Little bit
70 Fair-hiring org.

DOWN

1 River regulator
2 Genetic stuff
3 Opens, as a gate
4 Hajji's destination
5 Proceed à la Captain Kirk?
6 Nimitz or Halsey: Abbr.
7 Glittering, like a diamond
8 Latin 101 verb
9 It's no bull
10 Wombs
11 Archaeologist's find
12 Free of problems
15 "Have ___ and a smile" (old slogan)
18 Wine: Prefix
19 Paint crudely
23 Plumlike fruits
24 Mtn. stat
25 Fiber source
26 Radio personality ___ Quivers
27 Repeated words in a famous soliloquy
31 Narc's discovery
33 Hamilton's bill
35 Fundamentally
36 Group values
37 Tibia's locale
39 Doc's needle
40 Half an Orkan farewell
41 Forest name
46 From the top
47 Ex-champ Mike
49 Antiquing agent
51 Capital of Ghana
52 Frasier's brother
53 Whistle blasts
54 Special Forces cap
55 Wipe clean
60 PC component
61 Ring victories, for short
62 Malay Peninsula's Isthmus of ___
63 Gloppy stuff
64 List ender

by M. Francis Vuolo

ACROSS

1 La ___, Calif.
6 George Michael's old musical group
10 Shuts up, as a hostage
14 Having a line of rotation
15 Sword handle
16 Sea eagle
17 Mild, white cheese
19 ___ tide
20 Cain's victim
21 Video arcade name
22 Dracula portrayer
26 Radio knob
28 Apprised (of)
29 Twenty: Prefix
30 Miss Piggy's question
31 Partner of life
35 List concluder
36 More than a short story
40 August birth, most likely
41 Ship's trail
43 Niece, e.g.: Abbr.
44 Sham
46 Shipment to Detroit
48 Disburses
49 Three time N.L. M.V.P.
53 "Let's Make ___"
54 Foodie Greene
55 Hashish source
56 Lively folk dance
62 Fit to ___
63 Needle case
64 Studio sign
65 Sole
66 Steno's product
67 Link

DOWN

1 Rush hour feature
2 Nonwinning tic-tac-toe line
3 Columnist Smith
4 "Give me your tired . . ." poet
5 George Wallace, e.g.
6 Marine snail
7 "2001" computer
8 C.I.O. beginning
9 Transit of song
10 Polite
11 Of a surface
12 Make twisted
13 Photo color
18 French president Coty
21 Cabinet dept.
22 Shepherd's charge
23 Thin plate, anatomically
24 Army problem
25 Catch, slangily
26 Vista
27 Eight: Prefix
32 Actress Massey
33 Darn
34 Lads
37 City near Utah Lake
38 Agnew, once
39 Wisconsin city, childhood home of Harry Houdini
42 Loose nut?
45 Greek
47 Chess champ Mikhail
48 Mr. Connery
49 Auto racing's Bobby
50 Schiller's "___ Joy"
51 Gulf of Aden land
52 Writer Marsh
56 Pro ___
57 Consumed
58 Pirate drink
59 West Coast airport, briefly
60 N.Y.C. school
61 ___ gratia artis

by David J. Kahn

72

ACROSS

1 Impressionist Edgar
6 Phrase of understanding
10 Dan Blocker TV role
14 It may be blessed
15 Make airtight
16 Ready for business
17 "American Graffiti" actress
19 Alliance since 1949
20 Myrmecologist's subject
21 Ring of water
22 Bray
24 Thailand, once
25 "Richard ___" (E.A. Robinson poem)
26 Embroidery yarn
29 Top notch in ratings
33 Hounds' prey
34 Unexpected advantage
35 Coax
36 Rose's lover, on Broadway
37 Might
38 Intl. relief org.
39 Warsaw ___
40 Back muscles, for short
41 Irving Berlin's "Blue ___"
42 Linksman Craig et al.
44 Singer Rudy
45 Use the library
46 Time starter
47 Rock dove
50 Eagerly expecting
51 Cultural Revolution leader
54 Battle song
55 1963 chart topper
58 0 on the Beaufort scale
59 Geraint's wife
60 1935 Triple Crown winner
61 Means justifier
62 Parsnip, e.g.
63 Meddlesome

DOWN

1 Prefix with -hedron
2 Novelist Hunter
3 Urbane fellow
4 Common conjunction
5 Blocks
6 Malcolm X's faith
7 Pants part
8 Musical skill
9 Norwegian dog
10 Fragrant flower
11 Brightly colored fish
12 Bristle
13 Bamboozle
18 Fossil fuel
23 Flub
24 1985 Jessica Lange film
25 Chills
26 Wrangler's wear
27 Morocco's capital
28 Susan Lucci soap role
29 Hall of Fame QB Dan
30 Follow
31 See eye to eye
32 Pee Wee ___
34 Partner of room
37 Comet, e.g.
41 Ralph of the N.B.A.
43 Sign after Cancer
44 ___ dire (jurors' examination)
46 München, e.g.
47 Tempo
48 OPEC member
49 Aurify
50 Exchange premium
51 "Serpico" author Peter
52 Persistent pain
53 Approve
56 Popular card game
57 Med. insurance plan

by Gregory E. Paul

ACROSS

1. ___ tunnel syndrome
7. Less lenient
14. Feudal tax
15. One "T" of TNT
16. Big wheel in Moscow?
18. Doctrine: Suffix
19. Striped
20. Marry
21. "Miss ___ Regrets"
23. Comedian Louis
24. Actress Anderson
25. Former capital of Alaska
27. Airline to Stockholm
30. Commedia dell' ___
31. Canton cab?
35. "___ Te Ching" (classic work by Lao-Tzu)
36. "Ben ___"
37. A well-made fez, for example?
45. Fencing tool
46. ___ man (unanimously)
47. Scimitar
49. Put safely away
50. W.W. II fliers
53. Addict
54. Word of advice
55. Mohammed's daughter and namesakes
59. Mao ___-tung
60. Chattanooga choo-choo?
63. Apartment dwellers
64. 1964 pop sensation
65. Ancient ascetics
66. Size up

DOWN

1. Severely critical
2. 1928's Happy Warrior
3. Literary monogram
4. Bucket
5. Once more
6. Baseball's Dykstra
7. Greek portico
8. Recommend publicly
9. Pronoun for a Parisienne
10. Wish otherwise
11. ABC or FOX, e.g.
12. ___ cordiale
13. Less robust, as a musical sound
14. Certain chamber groups
17. Singer Della
22. Schuss
24. Fond du ___ Wis.
26. No voter
28. Reason for balm
29. Synagogue
32. Compass point
33. Palace Theatre locàle
34. Discordant deity
37. Having a will
38. Periods when the computers work
39. Takes down the "Closed" sign
40. London's ___ Gardens
41. "Mack the Knife" singer
42. Sch. near the White House
43. Inns
44. Locks
48. Attire
51. Microscopic creature
52. Modern messages
55. Huckleberry ___
56. Entr' ___
57. Source for Pravda
58. Bath and Baden-Baden
61. "Norma ___"
62. Hwy.

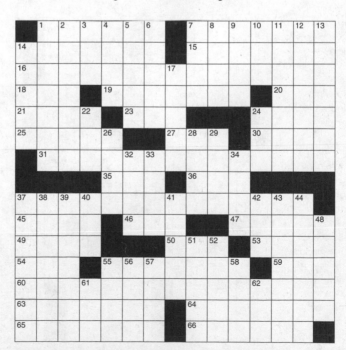

by Christopher Page

ACROSS
1 Handed out
6 Ditto
10 ___ Raton, Fla.
14 Goldbrick
15 Wallet fillers
16 Peepers
17 Actress Diamond
18 Fender flaw
19 Pronto
20 Manhattan, for one
23 Poetic monogram
24 Tiny powerhouse
25 Modeling agency executive Ford
27 Foe of the Philistines
30 RV
32 "Rumble in the Jungle" boxer
33 Changed the décor
35 Krupp works city
38 Assign places to
40 Alpine song
42 Ophthalmologist's case
43 Greek Pax
45 Palindromic principle
47 Before, to Browning
48 Plumber's need
50 Enjoyed a wad of tobacco
52 Flatter, with "up"
54 Impulse
55 Miscalculate
56 Crème gauloise, today
62 Columbia student
64 Rockies resort
65 Fish served amandine
66 Narrow way
67 Actress Sommer
68 By and by

69 "___ Rather Be With Me" (1967 hit)
70 Satyr's stare
71 Please no end

DOWN
1 Part of D.J.
2 Cather biographer Leon
3 "___ vostra salute" (Italian toast)
4 Logical premises
5 Tiller puller
6 Sinful city
7 De novo
8 Fix
9 Prize
10 "___ sport . . ."
11 Christmas Eve dish
12 Halt
13 Quaking ___
21 "___, I'm home!" (sitcom opener)
22 Mature
26 Not so much
27 Draped dress
28 Former orchard spray
29 Trattoria treat
30 Autumn drink
31 Yemen port
34 Love excessively, with "on"
36 Rochester's beloved
37 Must have
39 Group of toads
41 Nobelist Walesa et al.
44 Hgt.
46 Meadow bloom

49 Nonsense
51 Ethically neutral
52 Poe poem, with "The"
53 Dickens's ___ Heep
54 "Ben-Hur" director William
57 Racer Yarborough
58 Quarterback's bark
59 Scintilla
60 Kind of pudding
61 To be, to Satie
63 Actor Beatty

by Gregory E. Paul

75

ACROSS
1 Mangle
5 Palindromic exclamation
8 The Mad ___
14 Magic phrase starter
15 Septuagenarian's kitty, for short
16 Shoe part
17 Leave in a hurry
19 Twisted
20 Say again
21 Actress North and others
22 Throbs
24 Where pins are made
27 Guarantee
28 Triple A handout
31 Sharp as ___
33 1st Earl of Beaconsfield
36 Navajo "hello"
38 Nonstick coating
39 Popular citrus drink
42 Forepart
43 "Dear ___"
44 Greedy eater
47 Vietnam's ___ Dinh Diem
48 Cruel
50 Pampers
53 Error
58 Kind of punch
59 Slightly later than optimal
60 Fold of skin under the throat
61 Ruby, e.g.
62 Military subdivision
63 Liabilities opposites
64 ___ la-la
65 Computer info quantity

DOWN
1 Half of a Hawaiian fish
2 "Isn't that ___ much?"
3 Spur
4 Cowardly Lion actor
5 Gap
6 Mountain gazelles
7 Shakespearean prince
8 Type of gas
9 A year in Provence
10 Ivan and Nicholas
11 Ripped or zipped
12 International fashion magazine
13 Actor Fernando et al.
18 Start the beer bust
21 Indian dress
23 South, in Soissons
24 Minnesota clinic founders
25 Computer game maker
26 Mongol tribesman
28 Breakfast fruit
29 Onward
30 Spotted horse
32 100 yrs.
34 Invigorate
35 It's south of Eur.
37 Sneakers type
40 Entre ___
41 Provide with weapons
45 More like overripe meat
46 Puzzle
48 Carpet fiber
49 ___ the job (inexperienced)
50 Closing musical passage
51 Snake eyes
52 Stitches
54 Ticket part
55 Like Albee's Alice
56 Send forth
57 Much is done for his sake
59 Elev.

by Susan Smith

1

```
S A G E   A M P S     P A S H A
A T O M   M A A M     A M A I N
L O O T   U L N A     R O N D O
A N D   E L L E R Y Q U E E N
D E M O T E     T O U R
    A R C T I C   D E S C R Y
D I N A H   C A D E T   A Y E
A G A L   M O D E L   D R A W
D O C   T O N G A   A E O N S
S T E R E O   E N A M E L
    A R L O     C O M E D Y
W O L F M A N J A C K   K O O
A M A T I   I A G O   M I N K
R I V E T   O N E S   A N N E
S T A R E   N E S T   E G A D
```

2

```
R E D P E P P E R     A P H I D
I R R A D I A T E   G R E C O
C H A R G E D A F F A I R E S
H A W S E R       L I M I T
E R L E   S I M O N   T O W
R D S   S E E S A W   L A N A
    B A R T O K   S O G G Y
    B E L L E S L E T T R E S
T R Y I T   H A W A I I
S E E P   H O T A I R   C P O
P A P   L A T E R   G A R R
    T I T U S     D A R R I N
C H E R C H E Z L A F E M M E
D E C O R   G O O N A T E A R
C R E T E   G E N E R A L L Y
```

3

```
O S L O   P A T E S   S T A G
F L A P   A W A K E   L O L A
F I V E S T A R G E N E R A L
S T A R T E R S   D E P O N E
    A R N E   P I C T
C A S T E S   L E E K   T E T
E T H O S   O A R S   P E R E
S T A R S A N D S T R I P E S
T A N S   I S E E   E L E C T
A R K   B R E D   A S S E T S
    M O L T   F L E E
T I V O L I   S A T A N I S T
S T A R O F B E T H L E H E M
A S I S   T E A S E   R O T E
R A L E   S A M O A   S P A N
```

4

```
A S T A   T E R N   O P A R T
M E A L   K N E E   V I R E O
P A P A D O C D U V A L I E R
S T E R E   H O R A   S A F E
    M Y R A   A L A N
S O B S   U N C L E R E M U S
A T E   M E T H   T I R A N A
M A G D A   S I P   E S S A Y
O R I E N T   N A G S   O P S
A U N T I E M A M E   U N T O
    H A L O   P L A T
A G A R   I D E E   R A N T O
D R J O Y C E B R O T H E R S
D I A N A   M R E D   A N I L
S T R E P   S O R E   N E M O
```

5

```
H A R P S   A B E E   M E A D
A D I E U   C E L T   I S L E
H O T O N T H E H E E L S O F
A G E N D A   B I R D D O G
    A D E   N E E
H E R H E A R T W A S W A R M
A R O O   R O I L S   C I A
V A M P S   A N S   A G E N T
O T E   T O T I E   E R S E
C O O L A S A C U C U M B E R
    A T H   P U N
  S T R I K E S   B I A F R A
P O U R C O L D W A T E R O N
A I N U   S L A Y   E R E C T
S L A P   H A K E   S O D A S
```

6

```
M E L E E ■ F A C T ■ ■ T A S K
A C A S E ■ A M O R ■ ■ A R L O
T H I C K J U I C Y S T E A K
H O R A ■ U N D O ■ H A S T O
■ ■ ■ P A D ■ ■ ■ K I M ■ ■ ■
F R I E D O N I O N R I N G S
R A T E S ■ A S H O T ■ A H A
A N T S ■ B F L A T ■ G I A N
N C O ■ C A T E R ■ M E A N T
C H O C O L A T E S U N D A E
■ ■ ■ A M I ■ ■ ■ E G O ■ ■ ■
S H A R I ■ F I J I ■ V A N E
H I G H C H O L E S T E R O L
O R E O ■ E X I T ■ U S E R S
W E E P ■ N Y E T ■ B E A M E
```

7

```
A S P E N ■ D A L I ■ A M I D
T H E S E ■ E G A N ■ V I V A
T A S T E ■ M O T S ■ E L A N
■ G O O D N I G H T I R E N E
■ ■ ■ P L O ■ S E C ■ ■ ■ ■ ■
P A R ■ E L K E ■ P I E C E S
O R A L ■ A I L S ■ E R O D E
L O V E A N D M A R R I A G E
E M E N D ■ S E M I ■ S T E M
S A N D A L ■ R E S T ■ I R S
■ ■ ■ G A L ■ ■ ■ E O N ■ ■ ■
I L L B E S E E I N G Y O U
N E A R ■ T E R N ■ G L A R E
K A T E ■ E R I N ■ L O R D S
S K E W ■ D Y E S ■ E N S U E
```

8

```
C O R M ■ I N C A ■ S C R A P
O L I O ■ M E L D ■ A H O M E
M E N U ■ P A I L ■ S I M O N
M I S S M A R M E L S T E I N
A C E T I C ■ B R A E ■ ■ ■ ■
■ ■ ■ A T T U ■ T R E B L E
E V I C T ■ N A P E ■ T R O Y
W I S H Y O U W E R E H E R E
E L I E ■ L M N O ■ L O W E R
S E N S E D ■ N O E L ■ ■ ■ ■
■ ■ ■ L I S P ■ S N O R E S
W H E N W E M E E T A G A I N
R O M E O ■ E T T E ■ I N D O
A M I N O ■ W A R N ■ S T E R
P O L E D ■ S L E D ■ T O R T
```

9

```
D O R M ■ S E D E R ■ S A M P
A S T I ■ H A U T E ■ T R I O
T H E S P O R T O F K I N G S
E A S T E R L Y ■ A R R E S T
■ ■ ■ R A T S ■ A S I S ■ ■ ■
N A D I R S ■ P E T S ■ S T A
I D E A L ■ P A R E ■ O N E R
D A I L Y R A C I N G F O R M
E G G S ■ E P E E ■ A F O R E
S E N ■ S C A R ■ M I S T E D
■ ■ ■ A I R S ■ R I T E ■ ■ ■
S T A P L E ■ R E L E A S E S
W I N P L A C E A N D S H O W
A L T A ■ T R A D E ■ O O N A
P E E L ■ E I D E R ■ N O S Y
```

10

```
S E M I ■ G A L A S ■ A F A R
I R A Q ■ A L I C E ■ L U L U
F I R S T O F T H E M O N T H
T E E ■ A L I S ■ ■ I N T E R
■ ■ ■ F L E E ■ P I N E ■ ■ ■
C A L L E R ■ S E A N ■ S F C
A L O E ■ C O N G O ■ P E R
M I D D L E O F N O W H E R E
E G G ■ A R R A Y ■ ■ Y A M S
O N E ■ Y I P S ■ E S P R I T
■ ■ ■ S O N S ■ L U C E ■ ■ ■
W O O L F ■ T O G A ■ P I T
E N D O F T H E C E N T U R Y
S T O P ■ R O M A N ■ A M O R
T O R E ■ A P P L E ■ M A N E
```

11

```
A L G A . I D E A . T A R P
S E E D . S E W U P . E L I A
C A R O L I N E K E N N E D Y
A G A . U S E . G O O S E S .
P U L L S . B O L G E R . . .
. E D I T H . R A Y S . L E E
. F O R A . I N C . F E E L .
L E O N A R D O D A V I N C I
E R R S . P A L . S I N N . .
X E D . A O N E . S L A Y S .
. . E N M E S H . E L B O W .
M T E T N A . E S L . R U E .
R I C H A R D D R E Y F U S S
E T R E . X E R O X . I C E T
D O U R . B U S Y . T E D S .
```

12

```
B A H S . E N O S . . T H Y .
A L E E . A R E N A . W H E E
J O L L Y G R E E N G I A N T
A P P E A R S . . O R R S . .
. . N R A . D I N E D . . . .
G R E E N I N J U D G M E N T
R E X . N E A R S . A S I A .
E A C H . A S H . N E X T . .
A C H E . S T O A T . R I A .
T H E G R E E N M O N S T E R
. . Q U I N N . L E T . . . .
F U M E . S E R I A L S . . .
G R E E N B A C K D O L L A R
E A R N . M A R I O . L I S A
D T S . W H I T . S E T S . .
```

13

```
M A R I A . C A R A T . C A Y
A L O N G . O S A G E . A D O
T O M T E R R I F I C . T R U
C H A R . Y E S . T H E B A R
H A N O V E R . R A I L A G E
. . A S S . S T E A L . . . .
T I K I S . A V E . I L I E .
O V I N E . L I P . A N O D E
W E T S . M A R . R E U S E .
. T O T E D . S A M . . . . .
P A Y L O A D . A N S W E R S
O C H E R S . A W E . A L O E
P T A . P U S S Y W I L L O W
P O W . O R A T E . A L E N E
A R K . R E T A R . M A N E D
```

14

```
. . . P A R S E . P E A R S .
C R A N I U M . A E S O P S .
R E R A T E S . C R E M A T E
A D E L E . R E O . A R A P .
S O S O . P L E D . S I E N A
. . G A L E N . R A N . . . .
I M A . V A N E . E L E V E N
L A W . A N A G R A M . I W O
K I N D L E . A E R O . M E G
. . R O T . D A M N S . . . .
C H A I N . D E M S . C R O P
L O P E . S I S . P R A D O .
U S E D C A R . S T R I P E D
. T R U D G E . I S O M E R S
. S P E A R . R E A P S . . .
```

15

```
C L O B B E R . S A L . F L O
D E S E R V E . C R A T I O N
S A L L I E D . I M P A S S E
. P O L A R O P P O S I T E S
. . E N S . E I R E . . . . .
M A G S . E G O . M O N A . .
A P R . E A R L . M A D D O G
C H I L L Y R E C E P T I O N
H I P P I E . G A L E . U N E
O D E S . M G M . A M E S . .
. . W H E E . I A N . . . . .
C O O L H E A D E D N E S S .
O N G O I N G . R E D M E A T
K I R S T I E . L A R I A T S
E N E . E E R . E L E C T E E
```

16

USAF CAST ABBA
HARI RIPUP PLOY
FATSDOMINO RAGE
RICO KITH CIA
CHUBBYCHECKER
THEBAY SERA
CHORTLED REMOVE
OAK SOD RAT
DREAMT CALABASH
YURI MALONE
SKINNYDIPPING
HER ISAR BAER
ONES THETHINMAN
CYST SONAR ZERO
KATE SENS ANEW

17

MAGUS HEMP BASS
OCALA ALAI ARIA
THENUDISTCOLONY
ELATED TAR LAS
SET SERAGLIO
ELF DOOM DNA
RARE URIS GLOB
GROVERCLEVELAND
AMEN HITE OKAY
RAF NERO SIE
IMCOMING IDA
OAR EGO STELLA
THEBLARNEYSTONE
AREA RACE SOLTI
SEPT ODOR ANAIS

18

DEBRA PLACE ABE
ARLES CONAN RED
FRENCHTOAST ENG
NESTEA STARGAZE
EDS TLC BAA
ITALIANHERO
JAM CELEB TAKER
OPAL RIVET NEAL
GOTUP PERIL DRY
SPANISHRICE
ACT ATE QBS
DISRAELI ACTUAL
ROT SWISSCHEESE
ANY SETTO ELLIE
WAX ODEON RELET

19

MEHTA GASLAMP
MAYORS TALLULAH
ANEMIA OBLIGATE
RECAP SNEAD NEW
AGEING YET
RATE DAUBS AJAR
UPC LEPER RIATA
MPH CASTOFF WIN
PLEAD OWNED BLT
SERB ONICE ARTS
COG SOLACE
ASK FLATS SCARS
DOESTIME KOOKIE
DARKENER INSECT
SPRINGS METRO

20

BASEL AMIS BALS
ADALE RANT IMON
TEXAS ANDA SODA
ELOPER AIRSTRIP
DENS ONTARIO
ERNIE DUAL
MVP ANTE DERMIS
GEORGIA NEWYORK
SECEDE SOFA SAY
ROTO TREYS
ALABAMA ASEA
SPOILERS TENETS
PENN SASE IDAHO
RACE OVER NOTON
YSER PONE EROSE

21

```
 CASTANET LIFT 
DALAILAMA EGRET 
ANTIPASTO AGILE 
UTE SPA PRICER
BORSTAL PENNAME
  LES CARESSES
 SAAR POLED STA
MARY CARES TEES
INT POPES PIER
STIMULUS DIN 
LACONIA PRESIDE
ECHOIC HOR GOV
AROSE PROVOLONE
DUKES ABNEGATES
 ZEST DIESIRAE
```

22

```
ABCS CARUSO JAR
RILL OPENED UMA
CLAUDERAINS DAM
SKYGOD PTA ADZE
  LIS STEPHEN
UNJILTED ELOI 
ROAN OWEN OGRES
SECT REMIT ESSO
ASKEW RONA ECTO
 LAIC BANKSHOT
EMERGES SKA 
LAMS TOE ASIANS
ISM JEFFBRIDGES
ZOO ORATED OUST
ANN BASSES LESS
```

23

```
LASH EDGAR BRAT
ASKA SARTO ROTH
WHATSTHATYOUSAY
NOTRE DIARIST 
SWEARAT CLASP 
 CARAT TEENS
PECK OLIO ORRIN
ETO IWONDER OKA
STUDS NEED STEP
TUNIS DUNCE 
 SMUTS MAHALIA
 REPEATS ICONS
WELLSHUTMYMOUTH
OBOE OREAD WIRE
WARD EMMYS SEAN
```

24

```
GALAS FUM JOKER
ALEUT ITO OVINE
MEANY FAD TETON
YERTLETHETURTLE
 IONE MINH 
LUBE DER THEONE
ANO HONED EASEL
IFIRANTHECIRCUS
RESOW HARUM ARA
SDEATH BIT EROS
 SHAG VEAL 
HORTONHEARSAWHO
ACTER ORB TIEUP
STERN SIL ANDRE
POSSE TEE RESTS
```

25

```
WARPATH UPSCALE
ELECTEE GEORGIA
SANTANA LAWYERS
TNT EDDY ESSAY
 BYTHE ART 
MELEE UMPS ABEL
EXALT NOAH LOLA
CELLIST GETBUSY
CRAB PETE RATIO
ATWO ARAT OLSEN
 TIM PUPIL 
SCOTS VERA IRA
HEROINE NICEGUY
ADAMANT ENCLOSE
WELSHES RECITES
```

26

```
S T R O P   S P A   S M A S H
C I A N O   A I D   L I M P Y
O T T E R   L E D   A X I O M
W H O L E W A T E R M E L O N
L E N O   A Z A N A   D E N S
      I O N A   D I N G
S P E N C E R   A D O R N E D
C U L P A       R E U S E
I N S O L E S   A S S E N T S
    R A N T   S T E N
O I N K   C A S T E   S A P S
C H I C K E N T A R R A G O N
T O T H E   D O R   A L I N E
A P R O N   E A T   V A N C E
D E E P S   E T E   E D G E R
```

27

```
A M A T I   A M I E   S E T S
R U N I N   B O O S   T R I O
K N O C K A B O U T   R I L L
S I N   B L E D   I C I C L E
      B L A S   A M O K
C E L L O S   T R A D E W A R
E L I O T   H I R T   F A T A
S L O W   H E N I E   O L A V
A I N T   O A T S   F R E R E
R E S O U N D S   T O C S I N
      R T E S   L O R E
P R I C E Y   I O T A   D U E
R I C H   P U N C H B O A R D
A L O E   O R C A   I C I N G
Y E N S   T E A L   T A S S E
```

28

```
C A P P   M A A M   S P A K E
O D O R   O U R S   W A N L Y
M U S E   O N E S   A L G E R
B E T T E R T O   E T A L I I
    P E A   L I G H T O N E
A L O N G S   A D O S E
C A N D L E   E L I   S P A N
I L E   E C O   E S S   E L O
D A D E   R U E   T H A N T O
    S P E C K   S A V I O R
C U R S E T H E   N E T
U S H E R S   D A R K N E S S
R U I N S   A O K I   U N I T
D A N C E   N U I T   E C T O
S L O E S   E T N A   S E E P
```

29

```
G O D   B U B B A   S N E A K
R A E   Y P R E S   T E R R E
A T M   D E A T H   R U I N G
S H O T I N T H E D A R K
      A N D S   A D O
  L A S T S   B A L A N C E D
R A T S O   S E L A   A R E
O U T O F T H E P I C T U R E
A R I   R A P S   R U S E S
R A C E W A Y S   R A T E D
      R E M   A U N T
  S N A P D E C I S I O N S
H O T E L   A G E N T   P I T
A N E S T   M A T E O   E N E
T E N T H   A D O R N   N E W
```

30

```
J A I L   E S P O S A   A T L
A I D E   S T O R A G E F E E
P R O D U C I N G X R A T E D
E E L   P O L E     T O N G
    S O R T   I M M E N S E
A C C E N T   S L O A N
L O A M   M A O R I   M A S
M O V I E S I S N O D O U B T
S T Y   M E N S A   P L E A
    M I N D Y   C H E E S Y
I N S E R T S   A R A N
P A T E     A M U R   H A Y
A R I S Q U E B U S I N E S S
S C R E E N T E S T   E R I E
S S S   D E A L E Y   W E A R
```

31

J	I	L	T		C	A	I	R	D		S	O	O	T
A	L	O	E		O	L	D	I	E		P	E	N	A
M	E	G	A		S	A	I	D	J	U	L	I	E	T
	T	O	R	O	M	E	O		E	T	A	L	I	I
		O	N	O			I	C	E	S				
I	F	Y	O	U		W	O	N	T	S	H	A	V	E
D	R	U	M	S		R	A	T	E		L	I	L	
L	I	C	S		P	O	K	E	D		D	I	A	L
E	T	C		O	N	E	R		A	R	E	N	A	
R	O	A	D	S	I	G	N	S		L	E	N	D	S
		E	E	N	S			C	S	A				
A	L	B	E	R	T		G	O	H	O	M	E	O	
B	U	R	M	A	S	H	A	V	E		S	A	M	S
E	R	I	E		T	I	L	E	S		U	T	A	H
T	E	E	D		O	P	E	N	S		P	A	N	E

32

B	A	C	H		C	H	I	C			S	H	A	G
A	S	I	A		H	A	S	H		S	K	I	L	L
S	H	A	N	G	R	I	L	A		P	U	L	S	E
		R	O	G	E	R			E	L	T	O	N	
S	A	L	A	A	M		M	E	A	L				
P	R	E	M	I	E	R	E		C	R	I	S	I	S
A	M	A	I	N		E	T	C	H		S	E	N	T
R	U	N	T		Y	A	H	O	O		L	A	V	E
T	R	E	Y		E	R	I	C		P	A	G	A	N
A	E	R	I	A	L		C	O	R	O	N	A	D	O
		S	U	L	U			A	D	D	L	E	S	
S	T	I	L	T		M	A	R	N	I				
H	A	G	A	R		B	R	I	G	A	D	O	O	N
I	R	O	N	Y		R	U	D	E		O	R	L	Y
N	A	R	D		A	G	E	D		C	O	D	E	

33

Q	U	A	F	F	S		J	A	Z	Z		A	B	S
U	P	R	O	O	T		O	B	O	E		L	A	C
E	S	S	E	N	E		C	O	R	R		I	T	O
		D	R	E	A	D	N	O	U	G	H	T		
R	A	P	T		E	L	S	E		M	A	N	E	T
I	N	R	E	V	O	L	T		L	O	W			
A	G	O	R	A		E	A	S	E	S		T	I	M
L	E	X	I	C	O	N		A	S	T	A	I	R	E
S	L	Y		U	P	S	E	T		E	L	M	E	R
		C	U	T		Q	U	I	L	T	I	N	G	
E	P	S	O	M		P	U	R	R		I	D	E	E
S	H	O	O	T	B	L	A	N	K	S				
S	A	C		U	R	A	L		I	T	A	L	I	C
A	S	K		B	A	I	L		N	A	M	E	L	Y
Y	E	S		E	D	D	Y		G	R	A	T	E	D

34

A	W	E	D			M	A	O		O	S	I	P	
L	O	V	E	L	Y		A	S	P		D	E	M	I
B	R	O	C	A	S		T	H	E	B	E	A	R	S
S	N	E	A	K	E	R		E	R	I	T	R	E	A
			P	E	R	I	L		A	G	T	S		
B	O	S	O	M		G	I	G		S	A	T	I	E
A	C	A	D	I	A		N	O	A	H		O	L	D
R	A	U		C	H	I	C	A	G	O		W	I	N
E	L	L		H	A	L	O		E	U	R	E	K	A
R	A	B	B	I		K	L	M		L	U	R	E	S
		E	E	G	S		N	E	E	D	S			
V	U	L	G	A	T	E		D	R	E	S	S	E	R
I	L	L	I	N	O	I	S		G	R	I	E	V	E
A	N	O	N		O	R	A		O	S	A	G	E	S
L	A	W	S		L	E	X			N	A	S	T	

35

S	I	Z	E		S	L	E	W		S	E	M	I	S
E	R	I	K		T	O	N	O		P	L	E	A	T
C	A	P	E	V	E	R	D	E		R	I	D	G	E
			O	N	E	S			I	X	I	O	N	
	A	C	T	I	O	N		C	O	N	I	C		
S	N	A	I	L	S		C	H	A	G	R	I	N	
A	G	R	E	E		L	A	I	R	S		N	O	R
G	O	D	S		W	E	L	D	S		M	E	T	E
S	R	I		E	A	G	L	E		C	O	H	A	N
	A	G	E	N	D	A	S		T	A	B	A	R	D
	A	N	G	E	L		C	R	U	S	T	Y		
H	E	N	R	I		W	O	O	S					
U	R	B	A	N		N	E	W	J	E	R	S	E	Y
S	T	A	G	E		A	R	E	A		A	P	S	E
K	E	Y	E	S		T	E	R	N		M	A	S	S

36

```
YANG . CAPS . CHASM
AMOR . ADUE . HADTO
ROTI . LIRA . ANZAC
DIALMFORMURDER .
. . . LASS . ROY . .
BEDECK . AWN . MATE
OLA . AISLE . ENOS
MINDONESPSANDQS
BAKE . MOTET . RUE
ESEL . ZIP . DONEES
. . TAO . MULE . . .
. EFOREXCELLENCE
AVAIL . ROLO . DAUB
VERDE . ALOU . EZRA
GROSS . YENS . DIEN
```

37

```
BESS . EDENS . BMOC
AMAT . LEGIT . URSA
LIAR . ELATE . TBAR
MRBELVEDERE . AGE
. . . AAA . REVISED
COMMUTER . OISE .
ARR . DOVER . LABOR
SCUD . REGAN . NABE
HANES . RIPON . LOA
. ISEE . STROLLER
RIVIERA . MOE . .
ITE . MRBOJANGLES
CARD . ALTAR . EARP
ALSO . TETRA . NINE
NYET . AROSE . DRED
```

38

```
MOSHE . CRIB . CAPE
ATEAM . HOAR . OXEN
THEHONEYMOONERS
TOMATO . BARR . .
. . ETCH . DEARIE
. AUDREYMEADOWS
HANG . EDMOND . LIS
ALTO . INS . ELLA
DEI . ANNALS . LILY
JACKIEGLEASON .
INSETS . SMUT . .
. . ACTA . LEGATE
JOETHEBARTENDER
UNTO . GENE . LAIRS
GOON . GLAD . ERNIE
```

39

```
MATES . COB . MUTI
AGORA . HOI . SITON
RUYLOPEZOPENING
CASE . OSE . EMILIO
. . . SOS . TRISECT
BISHOP . PIUS . .
ADIEU . SILK . FAUN
SICILIANDEFENSE
HOAR . COKE . RATES
. . KENO . FOREST
RAGTIME . SAG . .
ELAINE . ICI . ONAN
FOURKNIGHTSGAME
INGES . NOW . OLDER
TEES . NRA . BEANO
```

40

```
ALEC . FRANC . SPAS
ROTA . AEIOU . NEWT
CURRICULUMVITAE
STEPSIN . SLIDEIN
. . ELLER . ALERTS
DEEDEE . AGUA . .
ELLIS . ENID . VISA
ABLE . AGAVE . IDOL
DEEM . ROME . ACERB
. . ESSO . BLEATS
MABELL . KIROV .
APOLLOS . LINEMAN
PERSONANONGRATA
LANA . GROVE . SLOB
EKES . AIDES . ALMS
```

41

```
M A R A T ■ M E M O ■ A C I D
A L I C E ■ A R A B ■ S A V E
W I T H H O N O R S ■ S P A N
S T A T E D ■ S L E W ■ A N T
■ ■ ■ E E R ■ A S H E N ■ ■
C A B ■ S I P ■ S E N D U P
A L A E ■ S A R G ■ A N G L E
C O N G R A T U L A T I O N S
A N D R E ■ A D A M ■ S W A K
O G L E R S ■ E R A ■ N E Y
■ E T A T S ■ E D S ■ ■
I R A ■ N I P S ■ O L E A T E
R E D S ■ G R A D U A T I O N
K N E E ■ M I L E ■ M O D U S
S O R T ■ A G E S ■ S N A R E
```

42

```
A C H Y ■ B U F F S ■ H E R A
S H O E ■ U R I A H ■ A V O N
H O P A L O N G C A S S I D Y
■ R E S A Y ■ T R I P L E ■
W A N T S ■ S H O O T ■ E N D
E L O ■ T H O R N ■ B Y T E
S E T S S A I L ■ M E E S E
■ ■ S K I P S B A I L ■
M E A T Y ■ T E N T A C L E
A N T S ■ A H E A D ■ R I N
O T T ■ E V E R T ■ S P A C E
■ H E A L E D ■ R O O N E ■
J U M P I N G O F F P O I N T
A S P S ■ G E L I D ■ L U S H
B E T E ■ E D E N S ■ S M E E
```

43

```
P A P ■ T R U I S M ■ A L P S
I S R ■ A U B R E Y ■ P O R E
S H E ■ P R E A C H E R R O E
A E S O P ■ R E S E T ■ E M K
■ E K E D ■ R H I N O S ■
W I N S T O N G R O O M ■
A N T ■ S N O R E ■ S U C R E
A C E R ■ T R A L A ■ S L A M
C A R O B ■ A V A I L ■ I S M
■ B R I D E Y M U R P H Y
H E C T I C ■ S N O B ■
E E L ■ C E S T A ■ C O O P T
F R A N K C H U R C H ■ A L E
T I N E ■ A O R T A E ■ R O N
Y E G G ■ P O K E R S ■ D T S
```

44

```
H A H A ■ C H A N ■ A N T O N
O R A N ■ R O N A ■ R E A D E
J O H N N Y O N T H E S P O T
O W N S U P T O ■ O T T E R S
■ ■ D T S ■ W O E S ■ ■
D U B O I S ■ S I R S ■ S I T
O B O E S ■ E T N A ■ T O R O
G O O D T I M E C H A R L E Y
M A N S ■ T I N E ■ D I A N E
A T E ■ A S T O ■ M O O R E D
■ T R E S ■ M A R ■
A S S A I L ■ C A S E M E N T
J A C K O F A L L T R A D E S
A L O E S ■ V O T E ■ G I N A
M E T R O ■ A G A R ■ I T E R
```

45

```
S H O V E L E R S ■ G L A D E
C A F E T E R I A ■ R O L E X
O V E R H A N G S ■ A Q A B A
R E D Y E ■ H E R D ■ N O M
E T E ■ L A S T B U S ■ A N I
D O N S ■ B E T O N ■ F L A N
■ P L U T O ■ S A D I E
S T R A I G H T F O R W A R D
A W O R D ■ H A D O N ■
L O S E ■ O D E T O ■ S S T S
A T E ■ E L O P E R S ■ T A P
D O A ■ P A G O ■ A D O B E
B O N Z O ■ M I R A B E L L A
A N N E X ■ A N N M I L L E R
R E E D Y ■ S T A I N L E S S
```

46

```
S A T E . . A T L A W . D H O W
I M U S . . M I A M I . R O M E
N I T S . . A N G E L . O R N E
E S T . . E T T E . L E O N I D
W H I P P O O R W I L L . . . .
. . . O I L . . A W E S O M E .
S K A L . . A S S A M . . L O U
W I L L O W T I T W I L L O W .
A R A . N I O B E . . W A G E .
P I N B A L L . . T W O . . . .
. . . W I L L O T H E W I S P .
S A F A R I . P A R E . D A R .
O P E N . A N I S E . M I N I .
M E T A . M A N T A . R O T O .
E X E S . S P E E D . S T A R .
```

47

```
A D O . A S H . . . H U H U H
M A R K S P I T Z . A T O N E
I N D O N E S I A . S A N T A
. . . J E A N S H E P H E R D
E M B A R K . A N N . . S U E
L O O K . . . . . T E S T E D
F A N . A L L S T A R S . . .
. B O N N I E P O I N T E R .
. . B E N D A B L E . D O G .
L O C A T E . . . . D I V A .
O R A . A H A . E M O T E D .
B A R B A R A B O X E R . . .
B L E A R . D O N A T I O N S
E L E N A . J O E C O C K E R
D Y N E L . . A T O . S O O .
```

48

```
C P L S . M A A M . C H O P S
U H O H . O N L Y . A E G I S
D E C I . T E A S . M A L E S
. W I N D O W S H O P P E R .
. . Y A R . I D E S . . . . .
T E E N Y B O P P E R . B B S
H A L O . U T E . S H O R T .
E G G S . S C R A M . O B I E
F L I E S . I D A . T U B E .
T E N . T A B L E H O P P E R
. . A I D A . J O E . . . . .
. P O P C O R N P O P P E R .
K A P O K . B E A N . P L U G
A C E R B . R I G G . E L M O
T E S T Y . A L E G . R A P T
```

49

```
J A P E . S A M B A . S W A P
A R I D . A L A I N . M O R E
W A N D E R L U S T . U N D O
S T A Y S A I L . A D D O N .
. . . . S H E . F O R G E R Y
H A W S E . D R I F T E R . .
A M I E N S . I F F Y . M O N
L I N T . A T S E A . P E L E
F E D . L U R E . L E R N E R
. E P I C E N E . L E T G O .
A R R I V E S . L I D . . . .
L U M P Y . P I N E T R E E .
E P E E . W U N D E R K I N D
C E R T . O S I E R . O M N I
S E E S . W E N D T . S E A T
```

50

```
A D O R E . S H H . T R O O P
M O T E L . M I A . E A R L E
F L I P F L O P S A N D A L S
M E S A . O R P H A N . N I T
. . . S C R E E . H I N G E S
R A P T O R . S A S S Y . . .
E U R . W I D T H . S E D G E
F R E E B E E . A S H T R A Y
S A Y S O . M E T O O . E E R
. . . P Y L O N . M E D D L E
S T R O B E . C E A S E . . .
A R I . O N C A L L . L P G A
B E D R O O M S L I P P E R S
L E G I T . D E A . C H E E K
E D E N S . R D S . S I N G S
```

51

```
I D A S ■ A M P S ■ ■ M O P S
N O R M ■ C O R O T ■ A L E E
L E N O S N O E L S ■ Y E L L
A R E O L E ■ L E A D S O F F
■ S T Y ■ S U R R E Y ■ ■ ■
S A S H ■ A L D A S S A L A D
T U N ■ S L U E ■ I M A G E
O R A L I S M ■ P A R S N I P
R A R E E ■ D O S E ■ G T O
K L E E S L E E K S ■ P S A T
■ S T O R M Y ■ R E S ■ ■
W I S E A C R E ■ O U T L A W
E R I E ■ H A R T S T R A S H
R O L L ■ S T I L L ■ I N T O
E N O S ■ A T C O ■ E G I S
```

52

```
O M A N ■ M E S S ■ A R G O T
D A R E ■ O R A L ■ M A U R A
D O C U D R A M A ■ A V E R T
■ ■ T I E S ■ V A N E S S A
S P I R A L E D ■ M A N S ■
T O N A L ■ D R U B ■ S T A T
R I F L E S ■ I S L E ■ I D A
I S O ■ C H U N N E L ■ M O T
F E M ■ T A S K ■ S A H A R A
E D E N ■ P O U F ■ T A T E R
■ R U L E ■ P R A I S E R S
B E C A U S E ■ I N N S ■ ■
I C I N G ■ S P A N G L I S H
T R A C E ■ T E R I ■ E R I E
E U L E R ■ E A S E ■ S E X Y
```

53

```
H I F I ■ S H A G ■ S E W U P
A R O N ■ C O P E ■ W A I V E
M A S S ■ R O S E G A R D E N
A N T I N O D E ■ E N N E A D
S I E G E D ■ J O K E ■ ■
■ R H O ■ P O O L ■ S C A M
B A H T ■ R A D I O ■ T R I O
A D O ■ A P I N G ■ O N T
R U M P ■ L U S T Y ■ A S T O
K E E L ■ E A T S ■ M R S ■
■ A M I N ■ P A M P A S
E G G N O G ■ Q U A D R A N T
P O W E R H O U S E ■ E T T U
I N E R T ■ D I N A ■ S C A D
C E N S E ■ A Z A N ■ T H E Y
```

54

```
W I T S ■ H A T S ■ P H I L S
O T H O ■ A S H E ■ R E N E E
L E R O U G E E T L E N O I R
F R E T S ■ A U T O ■ ■ L A B
■ E Y E D ■ N E E D E D ■
I M F ■ S O F T ■ B O X C A R
S E A M ■ P R O A ■ D U A N E
L A C A G E A U X F O L L E S
A L E N E ■ U C L A ■ T I M E
M Y S E L F ■ H E R D ■ F O E
■ O T T A W A ■ R E D O ■
O A F ■ S I B S ■ A R R A Y
T H E L I T T L E P R I N C E
T E V I S ■ H E E L ■ P I T A
S M E L T ■ E S P Y ■ S A S H
```

55

```
P A R T S ■ L I A M ■ C O R N
C L O U T ■ A G U E ■ O L E O
B O B B Y S H O R T ■ T I N Y
S T E E L E ■ R A I L ■ V E E
■ ■ U A R ■ S E E S A W S
B A N I S T E R ■ R A T ■
A D A M ■ E G O N ■ P A R E E
R A B B I D A V I D S M A L L
S K E I N ■ L E N A ■ E V I L
■ B E D ■ D E M O N I Z E
A M P E R E S ■ S S N ■ ■
M O I ■ T A P S ■ E E R I E R
A W E E ■ R I C H L I T T L E
Z E T A ■ T R U E ■ D E C K S
E R A T ■ H E D Y ■ A S H O T
```

56

```
O L G A   E B O N   K A R A T
R O A M   L O R E   A M U S E
B U M B L E B E E   T I M O N
S T A L A G   O D A Y   B R O
      E V A S   Y O D E L E R
D I S S E N T S   K I N E
R O T   S C O T S   D I S C O
A L U M   E R E C T   D E A D
G A M I N   M I R E D   A P E
    B R O M   N A R R A T O R
C A L O R I E   P R I G
O N E   M A T S   I L L U S E
T I B I A   H U M B L E P I E
A T U R N   O R A L   A T A N
N A M E S   S E X Y   M O M S
```

57

```
    C D E   S A M A R   E D A
W R O T E   C R E P E   P A C
P U T O N T H E D O G   I L A
A S H I N E   I L L I C I T
    H E L E N S   C O E S
    L E A D A D O G S L I F E
D O I   D E K E   A N A T
E D N A   R E P O T   M D S E
N O D S   O T R A   I T S
T R Y I T O N T H E D O G
    D I R E   E N D U E S
S T D E N I S   C L I N I C
A H A   G O T O T H E D O G S
B O Z   E L L E R   S A U N A
E R E   D E E R E   S S E
```

58

```
A R G O N   R O A M S   B V D
S O U S A   A F L A T   L E E
T W I S T O F F A T E   I N A
R E D   E L F   E A R N E D
O R E M   E L M S   M A D R E
    A N G E R E D   D D A Y
  A F R O   S R A S   A T E
  L I T T L E M A N T A T E
F I R   A L T I   A L E S
R E S T   B E T T E R S
A N T I C   S H A Y   O B O E
M A R M O T   P E A   R A G
E T A   R O L L E R S K A T E
R E T   G A Y E R   H I K E S
S S E   I D E A S   E X E R T
```

59

```
R A N   C O M T E   A R M E E
A V A   O M A H A   N E A R S
T I D E W A T E R   A V I A N
A D A M A N T   L I C E N S E
      C R I E R   R I N S E S
N O S E D   S E V E N U P
I M P E L S   T O N   E R A T
P E R   Y E A R N E D   I R E
S N I P   C S A   S I N N E R
    N E M E S I S   S A G A N
B E G L A D   N E A T H
L A T I M E S   C L O U D E D
A R I C A   W A T E R M A I N
S E D A N   A P O R T   I R A
E D E N S   T O R T S   L E S
```

60

```
S W I P E   M E T S   A M E N
P A L E R   A T O P   N Y R O
A R L E N   R A T A   A F R O
M Y S W E E T L O R D   A O K
      E S P Y   T A P I R S
C O M E T S   S C A L E R
O R Y   S O R E L   I N L A W
P A L M   M Y W A Y   S A G E
S L E E T   N E P A L   D E A
    F E R B E R   L A W Y E R
D O T T I E   P I T A
E L F   M Y T H R E E S O N S
L E O S   O R E O   R A D I O
L A O S   N U L L   A B I N D
A N T S   D E L E   L I N E S
```

61

```
S T S . V E E P . S C I P I O
L E A . I A G O . T A B A R D
O X Y M O R O N . E T A L I I
B A S I L . S T E R N . S S E
S N O R E D . . N E A L . . .
. . O N O M A T O P O E I A .
R A P . T R I E R . S T R O P
A B E T . A N T A S . S I T E
J E E R S . A N N A S . S A D
A L L I T E R A T I O N . . .
. . . G A M E . S P E E D O .
A C T . T O T E M . R A T O N
C O O L I T . M E T A P H O R
E R M I N E . M A I N . A N Y
D E B U G S . A L P O . N E E
```

62

```
S C A P E . C A S A S . S A T
A L L E Y . U H H U H . T I E
W I L K E S B O O T H . U S N
N O S A L T . T W O . M A L E
. . . N E A T . C L A R E T .
T A J . S T E M . R E C T . .
O M A R S . R E P A I R M A N
D I C E . T R A I T . O I S E
D E O D O R A N T . I N L E T
. . B A R E . D O R M . L A S
B E A C O N . N A P S . . . .
R E S T . C P A . M O C H A S
A R T . P H I L I P S O U S A
C I O . H E L O T . T U L I P
E E R . I S L E S . S T A N S
```

63

```
B O R I C . A R C . L E A F S
A M I N O . G E L . A L L O T
S A N J O S E C A . G O P R O
I N S U L T . R E O . A L P .
L I E N . R E S E T S . C O P
S S S . F I X A T E . J I V E
. L A P E L . S A N E R . . .
. J O S E C A N S E C O . . .
T R A C T . B U I C K . . . .
R E N O . B A L L E T . T O P
A D E . N O V E L S . M O N A
U T E . O W E . T R A C E R .
M A Y L E . N O W A Y J O S E
A P R I L . G A Y . N O M E N
S E E P S . E K E . E R E C T
```

64

```
A T I T . M E L S . S P A I N
T O N E . A R U T . P A S T E
S T E N . R I C E . E R A S E
E A R T H S C I E N C E . . .
A L T H E A . D R E I . M A A
. . . S A L . A A R O N S . .
A S H . D A I L Y P L A N E T
S M E E . R I O . G E R E . .
W O R L D R E C O R D . T A R
A T T L E E . I A N . . . . .
N E Z . A P E D . C R E S T S
. G L O B E T H E A T R E . .
W H A L E . S L U E . T A I L
O I L E R . E T E S . E L E E
O P E N S . N A S T . N E S S
```

65

```
T A P S . A R I Z . S A L A D
A V E C . B O C A . A M A T I
B A T H . B L I P . C A N O E
. N E W O R L E A N S J A Z Z
. T R A Y . A R T E . . . . .
A G E . L O W . A L B . E S P
M A D D . I A N . S V E L T E
B R O O K L Y N D O D G E R S
E D U C E D . W Y N . O M O O
R E T . A R P . S S R . E N S
. . U R A L . K O N G . . . .
B A L T I M O R E C O L T S .
E Q U I P . F O X Y . M A U L
M U T T S . I S I S . E R I E
Y A Z O O . T E A T . C Y T O
```

66

B	A	B	E	S		A	B	E	A	M		M	R	S
I	L	O	N	A		B	E	R	R	A		I	I	I
B	E	S	O	M		B	E	A	L	L		G	A	G
S	C	H	U	B	E	R	T	S	E	I	G	H	T	H
			G	A	Y		H	E	N		E	T	A	T
S	I	G	H		E	C	O		E	I	N			
O	N	O		S	O	L	V	E		N	I	C	E	R
P	R	O	K	O	F	I	E	V	S	F	I	R	S	T
H	E	N	N	A		O	N	E	T	O		A	T	E
		O	K	S		S	R	I		A	M	E	S	
B	L	O	W		E	L	S		R	O	T			
B	E	R	N	S	T	E	I	N	S	T	H	I	R	D
G	O	B		A	T	A	X	Y		T	E	N	O	R
U	N	I		G	E	S	T	E		E	N	A	T	E
N	E	T		S	E	T	H	S		R	A	T	E	D

67

H	A	G	S		K	A	F	K	A		B	O	S	S
A	L	O	E		O	B	O	E	S		O	K	L	A
I	T	O	R		D	U	R	A	N	D	U	R	A	N
R	E	D	M	E	A	T		T	E	E	N	A	G	E
			Y	O	R	K		N	O	R	A	D		
M	A	G	N	A		T	O	N		L	E	W	I	S
U	N	O	S		G	U	T		B	E	R	A	T	E
M	N	O		M	A	T	A	D	O	R		L	E	N
P	A	D	R	E	S		B	E	G		A	L	M	S
S	L	Y	E	R		R	L	S		E	R	A	S	E
			A	G	R	E	E		F	L	A	W		
A	P	O	G	E	E	S		G	U	M	B	A	L	L
S	U	G	A	R	S	U	G	A	R			I	L	I	E
T	M	E	N		E	M	E	E	R		A	L	D	A
A	P	E	S		T	E	L	L	Y		N	A	S	H

68

G	A	G	S		E	T	O	N		A	C	R	I	D
O	N	L	Y		R	A	F	T		M	O	A	N	S
E	G	O	S		L	I	F	E		A	L	I	S	T
S	E	A	T	B	E	L	T	S		J	O	L	T	
A	L	T	E	R		L	O	T		O	R	B	I	T
T	A	S	M	A	N	I	A		E	R	M	I	N	E
			D	O	G	G	E	D		A	R	C	S	
F	I	F	T	Y	T	H	O	U	S	A	N	D	T	H
E	Z	R	A		S	T	O	R	E	S				
E	V	E	N	S	O		D	I	L	I	G	E	N	T
L	E	E	Z	A		A	S	P		D	E	T	O	O
	S	W	A	N		I	T	I	N	E	R	A	R	Y
S	T	I	N	T		N	A	D	A		A	L	T	O
C	I	L	I	A		T	R	E	S		R	I	O	T
H	A	L	A	S		I	T	S	A		D	A	N	A

69

F	L	A	P		J	O	B		B	I	S	C	A	Y
R	O	S	A		O	P	E		I	M	P	A	L	E
A	C	H	Y		E	E	N		P	A	U	S	E	S
T	H	E	T	H	I	R	D	D	E	G	R	E	E	
			V	I	S	A		O	D	I	N			
F	A	T		C	U	T	L	A	S	S		W	A	S
E	C	H	O		Z	O	O			T	R	Y	S	T
T	H	E	F	O	U	R	T	H	E	S	T	A	T	E
C	O	R	F	U		T	O	Y		E	T	R	E	
H	O	E		T	R	E	A	T	E	D		T	O	P
			S	L	U	G		S	T	E	P			
T	A	K	I	N	G	T	H	E	F	I	F	T	H	
E	R	R	A	N	D		R	O	E		X	R	A	Y
N	A	T	T	E	R		O	T	T		E	A	R	P
S	P	E	E	D	Y		I	S	H		L	U	T	E

70

D	R	U	M		B	A	G			A	C	U	R	A
A	N	N	E		O	D	E	A		M	O	T	E	L
M	A	L	C	O	L	M	M	C	D	O	W	E	L	L
		A	C	E	D		M	O	A			R	I	O
	S	T	A	N	L	E	Y	K	U	B	R	I	C	K
T	L	C		O	Y	L		E	B	R	O			
O	O	H	S		G	E	T		A	B	I	E	S	
B	E	E	T	H	O	V	E	N	S	N	I	N	T	H
E	S	S	A	Y		N	A	H		N	E	H	I	
			S	P	A	T		N	E	A		S	O	N
A	N	T	H	O	N	Y	B	U	R	G	E	S	S	
C	I	O		E	S	E		W	E	R	E			
C	L	O	C	K	W	O	R	K	O	R	A	N	G	E
R	E	T	R	O		N	E	R	O		S	C	O	T
A	S	S	T	S			T	A	D		E	E	O	C

71

```
J O L L A ■ W H A M ■ G A G S
A X I A L ■ H A F T ■ E R N E
M O Z Z A R E L L A ■ N E A P
■ A B E L ■ ■ A T A R I ■ ■
F R A N K L A N G E L L A ■ ■
V O L U M E ■ A W A R E ■ ■ ■
I C O S A ■ M O I ■ L I M B
E T C ■ N O V E L L A ■ L E O
W A K E ■ R E L ■ P H O N Y
■ S T E E L ■ S P E N D S
R O Y C A M P A N E L L A ■
A D E A L ■ G A E L ■ ■
H E M P ■ T A R A N T E L L A
A T E E ■ E T U I ■ O N A I R
L O N E ■ M E M O ■ N E X U S
```

72

```
D E G A S ■ I S E E ■ H O S S
E V E N T ■ S E A L ■ O P E N
C A N D Y C L A R K ■ N A T O
A N T ■ M O A T ■ H E E H A W
■ S I A M ■ C O R Y ■
C R E W E L ■ F O U R S T A R
H A R E S ■ B O O N ■ U R G E
A B I E ■ C O U L D ■ C A R E
P A C T ■ L A T S ■ S K I E S
S T A D L E R S ■ V A L L E E
■ R E A D ■ S O M E ■
P I G E O N ■ A T I P ■ M A O
A R I A ■ S U G A R S H A C K
C A L M ■ E N I D ■ O M A H A
E N D S ■ R O O T ■ N O S E Y
```

73

```
■ C A R P A L ■ S T E R N E R
T A L L A G E ■ T O L U E N E
R U S S I A N R O U L E T T E
I S M ■ L I N E A T E ■ W E D
O T I S ■ N Y E ■ L O N I
S I T K A ■ S A S ■ A R T E
■ C H I N E S E C H E C K E R
■ T A O ■ H U R ■
T U R K I S H D E L I G H T
E P E E ■ T O A ■ S W O R D
S T O W ■ R A F ■ U S E R
T I P ■ F A T I M A S ■ T S E
A M E R I C A N E X P R E S S
T E N A N T S ■ B E A T L E S
E S S E N E S ■ A S S E S S
```

74

```
D E A L T ■ S A M E ■ B O C A
I D L E R ■ O N E S ■ E Y E S
S E L M A ■ D E N T ■ A S A P
C L A M C H O W D E R ■ T S E
■ A T O M ■ E I L E E N
S A M S O N ■ C A M P E R ■
A L I ■ R E D I D ■ E S S E N
R A N K ■ Y O D E L ■ S T Y E
I R E N E ■ T E N E T ■ E R E
■ S O L D E R ■ C H A W E D
B U T T E R ■ W H I M ■
E R R ■ V I C H Y S S O I S E
L I O N ■ V A I L ■ T R O U T
L A N E ■ E L K E ■ L A T E R
S H E D ■ L E E R ■ E L A T E
```

75

```
M A U L ■ H A H ■ H A T T E R
A B R A ■ I R A ■ I N S O L E
H I G H T A I L ■ G N A R L Y
I T E R A T E ■ S H E R E E S
■ P U L S A T E S ■
M A T ■ A S S U R E ■ M A P
A T A C K ■ D I S R A E L I
Y A T E E H ■ T E F L O N
O R A N G I N A ■ F R O N T
S I R ■ G O R G E R ■ N G O
■ I N H U M A N E ■
C O S S E T S ■ M I S S T E P
O N E T W O ■ H I G H T I M E
D E W L A P ■ G E M ■ U N I T
A S S E T S ■ T R A ■ B Y T E
```